EASY-TO-MAKE CHILDREN'S FURNITURE

Also by David Stiles

Fun Projects for Dad and the Kids
Huts and Hideaways
The Tree House Book

EASY-TO-MAKE CHILDREN'S FURNITURE
BY DAVID STILES

with designs and illustrations by the author

Pantheon Books, New York

Anyone wishing to manufacture any of these designs should contact:
David Stiles
161 E. 91st St.
New York, N.Y. 10028

Library of Congress Cataloging in Publication Data
Stiles, David R
Easy-to-make children's furniture.
1. Children's furniture. I. Title.
TT197.5.C5S74   684.1   79-3310
ISBN 0-394-73871-3

Manufactured in the United States of America

First Edition

Design: Robert Aulicino
Photography: Joel Markman

For Jeanie, with love.

Acknowledgments

I would like to thank my wife, Jeanie, for her assistance in researching and writing this book, and to Jean Trusty for her help in organizing the first and the final drafts. I am also most grateful to my good friend MiMi Green for leading me to Pantheon.

I wish to thank Barbara Plumb, my editor at Pantheon, who believed in my initial idea for this book, and who has given me her continued support and encouragement.

I am also indebted to Bob Scudellari and Robert Aulicino for their helpful suggestions and their design and final layout of the book.

In addition, I would like to thank Formica Corp., Nevamar, Stanley Tools, and Black and Decker, who provided materials and tools so that I could actually test these projects while writing the book.

Finally, I wish to express my appreciation for the professional advice I received from Marty Dolgos and Jim Barringer.

Contents

SECTION 1: FIRST STEPS

Introduction

This book was inspired by frustration with the children's furniture and equipment available on the market today. My wife and I had just had a baby girl and had bought a new crib. Besides delivering the crib late and with a dent in it, the retail store neglected to include the instructions for assembling it. Out of the carton dropped an assortment of rods, screws, nuts, bolts, washers, and springs, all of which seemed to be of mysteriously inconsistent sizes. "Have no fear," said my wife. "My husband is an industrial designer and will have this thing together in no time!" Three hours later, sweat pouring off my forehead, having used every swear word I know, this industrial designer finally succeeded in assembling the crib. It seemed that every logical step taken turned out to be a wrong guess — particularly since the functions of the rods and springs were never explained. Only when I was finished did I understand how it worked. This was a valuable lesson for me, and one I kept in the back of my mind when designing the projects in this book.

Most books on do-it-yourself projects are written by professionals whose knowledge, skills, and equipment far exceed those of the amateur. This book is written by someone who is not a professional but a do-it-yourselfer like you. I assume, therefore, that like me you don't have a great deal of time, money, or tools to build these projects. On the other hand, if you are investing your time and effort to make something for your children you will want the finished product to be something you can be proud of, something your child will enjoy, something that will be lasting. Consequently, I have attempted to make the instructions and drawings in this book as understandable as possible. To make sure the instructions I've given are sound, I have built every project. Whenever possible, I've tested the project with a child (generally my own) and have made modifications whenever necessary.

Design

You may notice that most of the furniture shown here shares a common look. This is not an attempt to create a new style in the children's furniture market. The designs simply evolved, practically by themselves, and by following a few common-sense requirements.

The first requirement was that the piece of furniture or play object be *safe.* Consequently, wherever possible I have recommended that you round off all corners and edges to prevent injury to the child. This may seem logical, but to date I haven't found a single children's furniture manufacturer that has incorporated this feature into its line. You'll find when making any of these projects that it's practically impossible to cut plywood without creating a splintery edge. This problem is neatly solved by rounding off the edge with a file rasp and sandpaper.

The second requirement was that all the projects be easy to make utilizing a minimum amount of expensive tools. Although most of these projects are easier to make with an electric router, I have provided alternative solutions for those who can't afford to spend money on electric tools (see Drawers, pages 13–17, and How to Cut Plastic Laminate, pages 6–8).

The third requirement was that all the pieces of furniture be able to withstand a great deal of wear and be easy to clean. The natural solution was to put a plastic laminate (Formica) covering on all surfaces that get a great deal of wear. Of course, plastic laminate is expensive and requires an extra step at the end; however, it is worth it, since it requires no additional finishing or painting once it is applied and can easily be cleaned. You'll see that most of the designs have some exposed wood showing. This is done on purpose to give some relief from the slick look of plastic laminate and to give the pieces a feeling of warmth and life.

Of course, all of the designs in this book can be made without plastic laminate, and instructions are given on page 6 on how best to finish the wood with paint.

The fourth requirement was that, whenever possible, the piece could be easily made into something useful after it had outlived its original purpose. For example, the baby's changing table becomes a child's storage bin simply by taking it off the wall and adding casters. This helps to minimize the built-in obsolescence factor of children's furniture.

A Word About Safety

Much care was taken to insure the safety of the projects in this book for children. In most cases I exceeded the guidelines set forth by the American National Standard Toy Safety Bulletin PS 72–76. Plastic coatings were checked for toxicity, edges were rounded, hinges were redesigned to eliminate possible scissoring action, and contact cements were checked for flammability. It is of great importance to follow the directions carefully, eliminating wood splinters by sanding and sealing, and using common sense where unusual conditions exist.

Also, in regard to your own safety, all tools — both manual and power — can be dangerous if misused. It is important to use them with extreme care at all times. If you are using a tool — particularly a power tool — for the first time it would be wise to have an experienced person demonstrate proper usage. And remember to keep *all* tools out of the reach of children.

Tools You Will Need

To build most of the projects in this book you'll need only the most basic tools, listed below in order of importance.

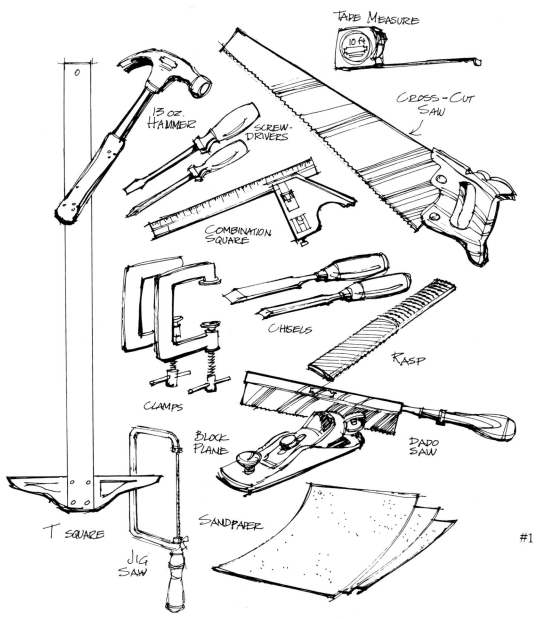

TAPE MEASURE

13 OZ. HAMMER

SCREW-DRIVERS

CROSS-CUT SAW

COMBINATION SQUARE

CHISELS

RASP

CLAMPS

BLOCK PLANE

DADO SAW

T SQUARE

SANDPAPER

JIG SAW

#1

Hand Tools

Hammer a 13 or 14 oz. claw hammer
Screwdrivers 1 medium size and
  1 Phillips-head type
Crosscut Saw 10 teeth (points) per inch
Tape Measure 1/2 in. wide, 8 ft. long
Combination Square with 45° angle
T-Square 48 in. long with 1 in. increments
Clamps 2; the jamb types are best
Wood Chisels 1/4 in. and 3/4 in. wide
Rasp Combination file and rasp—sometimes
  called "four in hand"
Jigsaw or Coping Saw (for cutting round
  corners)
Dado Saw 1 small 18 in. backsaw for small
  grooves and joints
Block Plane 6 in. long, used for trimming

Electric Tools

Electric 1/4 in. Drill with flat (spade) wood drill
  bits in sizes 1/4, 3/8, 1/2, 5/8, 3/4, and 1 in. Buy
  them as you need them. Although the electric
  drill is a somewhat expensive item, (approximately $20), I recommend that you buy it
  because a nonelectric hand drill can cost
  more. According to a recent survey, electric
  tools have not kept up with inflation over the
  past ten years. In fact, in some cases they cost
  even less than before. An electric drill is an
  indispensable tool to have around the house,
  even for the novice. It is also one of the safest
  electric tools you can own. Don't pay more
  money for a "reversible" motor, as you will
  rarely need this feature. Some electric drills
  come with variable speeds — a nice feature,
  especially for beginners, but not really necessary. Electric drills last a long time and are
  definitely a worthwhile investment.
Saber Saw Although most of the projects in this
  book can be made with a handsaw, it would
  save a lot of time and work if you have an electric saber saw. In this case it pays to buy the
  more expensive make; it will last much longer
  than a cheaper brand.
Sandpaper If you think all kinds of sandpaper are
  the same you probably haven't tried Garnet
  sandpaper (the same kind as on most emery
  boards). It is a reddish color, lasts at least five
  times longer than other sandpaper, and costs

THREE ELECTRIC TOOLS TO MAKE THE WORK EASIER

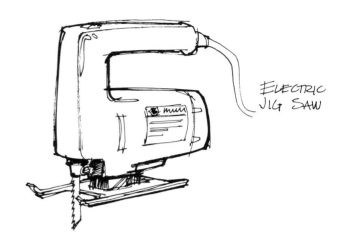

ELECTRIC JIG SAW

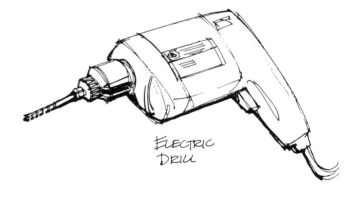

ELECTRIC DRILL

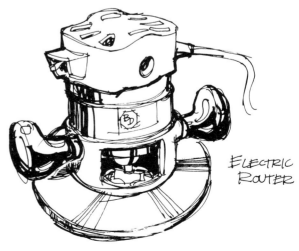

ELECTRIC ROUTER

#2

the same. For this reason it is often impossible to find in hardware stores. You can order it by writing to the Minnesota Woodworkers Supply Co., 21801 Industrial Boulevard, Rogers, Minnesota 55374. Ask for Garnet sandpaper made either by 3M or Carborundum. Order it in the following grades. You will need more coarse sheets than fine-grade sheets.

P2503	#120	Fine 31¢
P2505	#80	Medium 35¢
P2508	#50	Coarse 45¢

Router

An electric router is not an essential tool to have for making most of the projects in this book, but it is necessary if you want to make professional rabbet (shoulder) cuts or dado (grooves) (see illus. #3). The nice thing about a router is that it

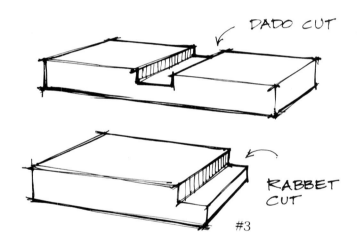

DADO CUT

RABBET CUT

#3

works quickly and makes a clean sharp cut that rarely requires additional sanding. It is relatively safe, as long as you use it according to the directions, but be prepared for a loud noise. Since it is not a tool you use every day, you should spend as little money on one as possible. However, if you plan to make more than five projects using a router, you should consider one in the price range of $40 to $50. In most cases, you should buy a router before you buy a table saw with a dado head. Be forewarned that once you buy the router you must also buy router bits, which often cost as much as the router itself. If you are cutting birch plywood you must use carbide bits; although more expensive, they save money in the long run. In place of a router you can buy a

simple dado or backhand saw and use it for your dado and rabbet cuts.

Portable Saw

It's surprising that portable electric saws (sometimes called circular saws or skill saws) are so popular. Although they do save time, they are rather frightening to use: they are loud, and they often buck, sometimes giving your wrist a sharp twist. Portable saws are, however, surprisingly cheap, often costing as little as $20. When there's a lot of cutting to be done they can save time.

How to Avoid Errors

Mistakes can be minimized by following a few basic rules.

1. Before cutting any wood, study the plans carefully and be sure you understand them. If you want to change the plans, make a scale drawing, one inch to the foot, indicating the change.
2. Check and double-check any extenuating circumstances that might affect the design of a project, such as whether it will fit through the door; whether it's the right size for your child; whether the project requires an expensive tool that you don't own.
3. Don't take *anything* for granted. When buying wood, check for warping, knots, dents, and cracks. Also measure the thickness. You may think you've bought a 3/4 in. thick piece of plywood and find, as I did on one occasion, that it's actually 1/16 in. less! Even stock lumber like 2 x 4s can vary from lumber mill to lumber mill. If the wood seems inordinately heavy to you it may be because it has not been seasoned (dried) long enough.
4. When measuring, make sure the tape is resting on the end of the tab and not on the little rivet that holds the tab.

When measuring for a long cut, make sure you mark four or five times across the width of the board with a pencil and connect these marks with a line drawn along a very straight board. It's a good idea to set aside a straight 1 x 4 just for this purpose.

Don't try to read your tape measure upside down. The numbers 29, 36, 46, etc. can be mistaken for 26, 36, 49, etc. Before cutting each piece, try to visualize how the piece fits into the others. Ask yourself if the size of the piece you are about to cut makes sense.

Wherever and whenever possible, don't rely on transferring measurements by using a ruler. For instance, if you've cut one side of a box out of a piece of stock, use it as a template for the others. If you need to cut four identical pieces of wood, use the first piece as a template for the next three, minus a pencil-line thickness.

Plastic Laminate Formica

Very few people use the words *plastic laminate*. Even hardware and lumber salesmen use the word *Formica* when referring to all the plastic laminate products. The word *Formica* is even in the dictionary as "a trademark for a laminated heat resistant thermosetting plastic used for table and sink tops, etc." There are over half a dozen manufacturers of plastic laminate whose product is quite similar to that of Formica's, and some with as good a selection of colors. Nevamar, for example, makes a "space blue" plastic laminate that was used on many of the projects in this book.

With all due respect to the Formica Corporation, the largest and oldest manufacturer of plastic laminate, I have used the term *plastic laminate* throughout this book. Plastic laminate is a by-product of World War II technology and has become popular among tradesmen over the years because of its high resistance to wear. Actually, plastic laminate simply consists of several layers of brown paper coated with plastic with a thin hard phenolic coating on the surface.

Painting vs. Plastic Laminate

Plastic laminate is recommended as a finish for most of the projects in this book because of its high resistance to wear and its cleanability. It is costly (approximately $1 per square foot or $32 a sheet in 1979), so it's important to compare the alternative of painting before making your decision. Keep in mind that you actually use less time to apply plastic laminate than to paint, because to do a professional paint job the wood must be filled with a spackling putty and sanded several times. Compare these steps:

Painting steps
1. Rough sanding
2. Spread with spackling compound putty and allow two hours to dry
3. Medium sanding
4. Repeat Step 2
5. Light sanding
6. Wipe with a tack cloth (a cloth dipped in a little paint thinner)
7. Paint and let dry three to six hours*
8. Light sanding
9. Wipe with tack cloth
10. Paint and let dry three to six hours*

* Spray horizontal surfaces only. When dry, turn object and repeat spraying.

Plastic laminate steps
1. Cut plastic laminate
2. Roll contact cement on both plywood and plastic laminate
3. Wait ten to fifteen minutes depending upon contact cement used
4. Lay plastic laminate onto plywood and press down
5. Trim off edge and you're done

Plastic laminate has generally been considered a material for professionals only, probably because it requires an electric router and expensive carbon-tipped bits to work it. Many professionals are accustomed to cutting plastic laminate with a table saw. Unless you are a professional and have a carbide-tipped blade and a special hold-down jig to keep the plastic laminate sheet from flying up into your face, I would not advise using that method. Plastic laminate can be cut with a $1.98 open end hacksaw or scored with a $2.00 carbide knife and snapped apart. Overlapping edges can be quickly removed with a small inexpensive hand rasp and finished with sandpaper. I first encountered this startling fact when I accidentally left all my power tools at another location and was suddenly hit by an urge to cover my drawing board with plastic laminate. By following the steps illustrated on this page, I was able to do a highly professional job.

How to Cut Plastic Laminate

Step 1. Lightly sand the surface of the material that you plan to laminate with rough sandpaper, making sure there are no splinters or protrusions which would keep the plastic laminate from lying flat. Lay the plastic laminate on the floor and, using a carbide knife and a metal straightedge, score the finished surface enough times to see the brown backing showing through the cut. Turn the plastic laminate over and score the back exactly along the same line as before (see illus. #4). Slip two long pieces of 1 x 2s nailed together to form a sharp protruding edge (illus. #5). Apply pressure to both sides by using long boards and snap it apart.

Step 2. When working with large pieces, cut the plastic laminate 1/4 in. larger than the actual piece so that there will be some room for error when placing it down.

Instead of a carbide knife you can also use an electric saber saw with a hacksaw blade in it, or professional plastic laminating shears, which chop a 1/4 in. wide swathe out of the plastic laminate. If you use a saber saw, which is the easiest, make sure to cut from the back so that the teeth are cutting against the finished side (illus. #6).

Plastic laminate, although strong in some

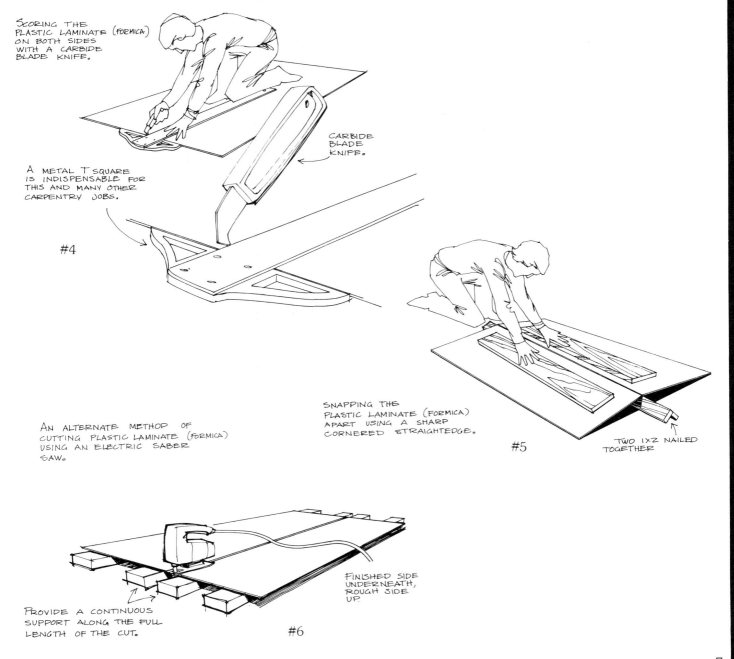

SCORING THE PLASTIC LAMINATE (FORMICA) ON BOTH SIDES WITH A CARBIDE BLADE KNIFE.

A METAL T SQUARE IS INDISPENSABLE FOR THIS AND MANY OTHER CARPENTRY JOBS.

#4

CARBIDE BLADE KNIFE.

SNAPPING THE PLASTIC LAMINATE (FORMICA) APART USING A SHARP CORNERED STRAIGHTEDGE.

#5

TWO 1X2 NAILED TOGETHER

AN ALTERNATE METHOD OF CUTTING PLASTIC LAMINATE (FORMICA) USING AN ELECTRIC SABER SAW.

PROVIDE A CONTINUOUS SUPPORT ALONG THE FULL LENGTH OF THE CUT.

#6

FINISHED SIDE UNDERNEATH, ROUGH SIDE UP.

respects, is very brittle and will easily crack or split unless supported 1/2 in. on both sides along the length of the cut while you are cutting it. Since you are going to trim off the edge later, you don't have to use a straightedge to guide it.

Contact Cement

The next step is to glue the plastic laminate to the surface of the plywood. Begin by dusting off any loose sawdust that may have collected. Following the directions on the can, liberally coat both surfaces of the plastic laminate and the wood with contact cement. If you have a large area to cover, try using a roller to apply the contact cement. The roller can be reused many times without needing to be cleaned.

Until 1977, commercially sold contact cement contained highly flammable properties. Personal experience proved how dangerous this type of contact cement was: Once, a gallon of it suddenly ignited in front of my face, set off by a small pilot light several feet away. The ensuing inferno completely destroyed my kitchen, and I barely escaped alive. Many lives have been lost and many people have been scarred and disfigured for life from using the old contact cement. There are many contact cements on the market now that conform to the new flammability codes, but avoid the water-base varieties since they don't hold as well. Be sure you have good ventilation. The problem with some contact cements is not the flammability but the noxious fumes.

Allow the contact cement to dry for the prescribed time (generally ten to forty-five minutes) and lay some 3/4 in. dowels on the coated wood, not more than 12 in. apart, to keep the two pieces from adhering to each other while you are aligning them (illus. #7). When you are sure there is an equal amount of overlap (1/4 in. on each side), press the plastic laminate down evenly and work up to the other end, removing dowels as you go along. When you have removed all the dowels, put the piece on the floor and jump lightly all over it while wearing soft-soled shoes like running or tennis shoes. Be sure the plastic laminate is pressed firmly to the plywood, especially at the edges (see illus. #8). If the piece you are laminating is over 2 ft. long and unsupported (as in a bookshelf), use another piece of plastic laminate on the underside to equalize the pres-

#7

THE EDGES OF PLASTIC LAMINATE ARE SOMETIMES DIFFICULT TO ADHERE. TO HELP PRESS THEM DOWN HARDER YOU CAN MAKE THIS SIMPLE TOOL.

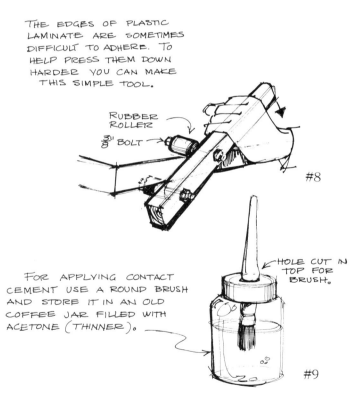

RUBBER ROLLER
3/8" BOLT

#8

FOR APPLYING CONTACT CEMENT USE A ROUND BRUSH AND STORE IT IN AN OLD COFFEE JAR FILLED WITH ACETONE (THINNER).

HOLE CUT IN TOP FOR BRUSH.

#9

sure; otherwise it might buckle later. If it is a small piece, you can use white glue, keeping it clamped or weighted to lay flat. Let it dry six to eight hours. Use a scrap of leftover plastic laminate to scrape off any cement that has accidentally stuck to the finished face of the plastic laminate. For average jobs, use a hand brush to apply the contact cement; store the brush in a jar filled with acetone (illus. #9).

Trimming the Edge

Trimming off the excess plastic laminate is no problem if you have an electric router. Simply insert a carbide rounding bit in the chuck of the router, set the depth, and round off the plastic laminate and the plywood in one operation (see illus. #10).

AN ELECTRIC ROUTER, ALTHOUGH NOT NECESSARY, MAKES THE JOB OF TRIMMING THE EDGE EASIER.

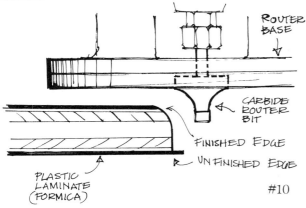

ROUTER BASE
CARBIDE ROUTER BIT
FINISHED EDGE
UNFINISHED EDGE
PLASTIC LAMINATE (FORMICA)

#10

If you don't own a router, you can still do a professional job by following these steps:

Step 1. Clamp the piece securely to a bench. With a four-in-hand or rasp, file the edge down. Always stroke away from the edge (not into it) to avoid accidentally lifting or scratching the plastic laminate (see illus. #11). Don't despair if at first

you get a very ragged edge. Keep working until you've exposed the top edge of plywood along the entire edge.

Step 2. Using a very small amount of contact cement, glue a coarse #50 piece of sandpaper to a piece of scrap wood 1 x 4 x 12 in. long. This sanding block is one of the best and least expensive tools you'll need for all the projects in this book; it enables you to do a highly professional job.

With both hands, hold the block lengthwise to the work and make long strokes back and forth (see illus. #12). In a very short time you will see

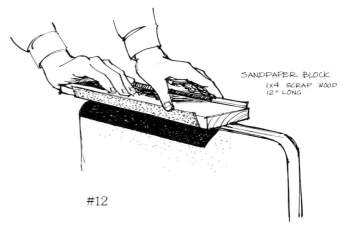

SANDPAPER BLOCK
1x4 SCRAP WOOD
12" LONG

#12

the edge become rounded. Switch to a medium #80 grade sandpaper and continue sanding until the edge of the plastic laminate becomes a constant straight line. File and sand the corners in the same way so that the curve (illus. #13) blends into the straight edge. Finish sanding with a fine #120 grade of sandpaper. When the project is completely built, give the edges three coats of polyurethane varnish.

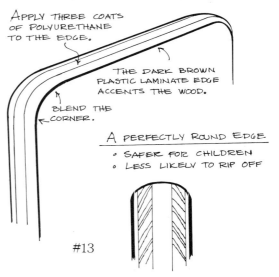

APPLY THREE COATS OF POLYURETHANE TO THE EDGE.

THE DARK BROWN PLASTIC LAMINATE EDGE ACCENTS THE WOOD.

BLEND THE CORNER.

A PERFECTLY ROUND EDGE
• SAFER FOR CHILDREN
• LESS LIKELY TO RIP OFF

#13

STROKE AWAY FROM EDGE

#11

Plywood

Buying Plywood

Since most of the projects in this book are made with plywood, you should familiarize yourself with the various kinds that are available. Plywood is made up of several layers of thin wood manufactured with the grain of adjacent layers at right angles to each other. The advantage over solid lumber is that larger widths are available with little or no warping.

Plywood is generally sold in 4 x 8 ft. sheets in 1/4, 3/8, 1/2, 5/8, and 3/4 in. thicknesses. It also comes in various grades: A/A for sheets with no blemishes on either side to A/D for sheets with one good side and one bad side. A/D is acceptable and is much cheaper than solid white pine.

Particle board is a possible alternative to plywood. It is more stable than plywood but is very heavy. Also, since it is unattractive, it must be covered with plastic laminate.

For a really beautiful job, use birch veneer (cabinet quality) plywood. Even this more expensive wood has a good and a bad side, so be sure to leave the good side exposed and cover the darker, inferior side with plastic laminate. Most plywoods have voids inside which become visible on the edges when you cut through the wood. This is unfortunate, and these holes must be filled with plastic wood or wood filler. Most of the projects in this book were made with birch veneer plywood. For an even better job, ask for "lumber core," which has solid wood inside instead of thin layers of wood.

For the ultimate in plywood, ask your lumber dealer to special-order thirteen-ply birch plywood (generally not stocked in most lumberyards). Most of this plywood is shipped from Europe and is very expensive.

Cutting Plywood

There are several ways to cut plywood, depending on your skill, experience, and tools. For the beginner, cutting a large piece of plywood into smaller pieces can be quite a problem.

Precut at the Lumberyard
The easiest way to cut up a sheet of plywood is to have the lumberyard do it for you. Most lumber-

yards offer this service and will charge you either a flat rate per sheet ($6 in 1979) or by the hour at $5 for fifteen minutes ($5 minimum). They often have a vertical wall-mounted saw that enables them to cut a sheet of plywood in just a few minutes. The disadvantage is that they will not guarantee accuracy of under 1/8 in., but you can usually compensate for this when you build. You must be absolutely sure of your dimensions before the wood is cut, and you must give the lumberyard an accurate sketch, called the cutting plan. This should be drawn to scale with a ruler, using a one-inch-equals-one-foot scale. You must allow for the kerf cut (material taken away by the saw blade) and indicate scrap by crosshatching (below). To figure out the most

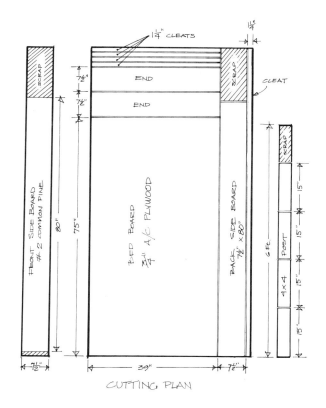

CUTTING PLAN

economical way of laying out the sheet for cutting, you may want to cut the pieces to scale out of paper and rearrange them on a 4 x 8 ft. rectangle also drawn on paper.

The advantages of having the lumberyard cut the wood is that all the pieces will have nice right-angle edges, you will have saved yourself an hour of work, and you will have eliminated the nuisance of getting sawdust over everything. In short, you will have avoided doing the hard work. To make it less confusing, write the dimensions and description of each piece on tape and ask the cutter at the lumberyard to attach the corresponding tape to each piece after it is cut. Since lumberyards can (and often do) make mistakes, be sure to check the measurements of each piece before you leave.

If you buy the plywood uncut, there remains the problem of how to get a heavy, 4 x 8 ft. sheet of plywood home. Many lumberyards will deliver free, but this requires a minimum order— sometimes over $75. Otherwise you will have to pay for delivery, or, if you have a car, you can pick it up yourself. A 4 x 8 ft. sheet of plywood won't fit inside most cars, but you can carry it on the roof of the car if you tie it down well. Bring along an old blanket to keep from scratching the roof and ask at the lumberyard for some heavy hemp cord. Use lots of it and crisscross over the top of the car, being sure to tie the plywood so

that it can't shift forward if you have to apply your brakes suddenly (see illus. #14).

Hand-Sawing
If you prefer to cut the plywood by hand, here are some tips to make the job easier.

Make sure your saw is sharp. The saw teeth should feel sharp to the touch. If they are not, take your saw to the hardware store or lumberyard and have it sharpened (approximately $5).

The most overlooked aspect of sawing a piece of plywood is how to support the wood while you're cutting it. A hand saw requires about a foot of clearance under the cut for the saw blade. This means you must support it on something rather tall while you are sawing. If you have two sawhorses you can start the cut at the far end and, as you get closer to the sawhorse, shift the plywood so the saw is in between the two sawhorses, continuing on toward the other sawhorse and then shifting again (see illus. #15).

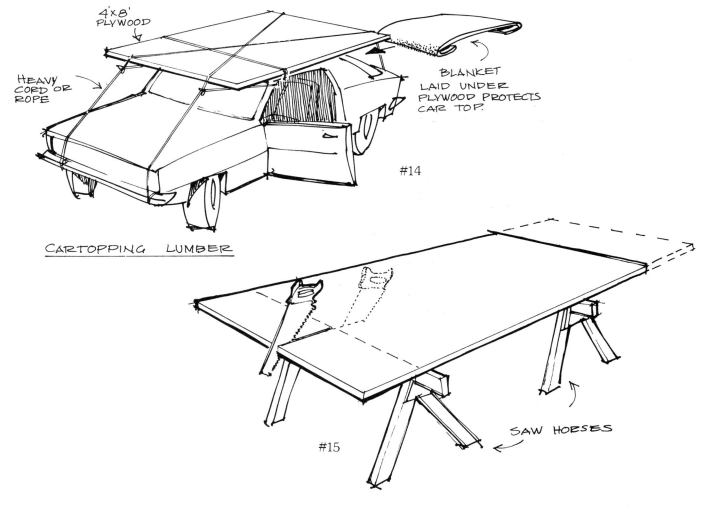

4'x8' PLYWOOD

HEAVY CORD OR ROPE

BLANKET LAID UNDER PLYWOOD PROTECTS CAR TOP.

#14

CARTOPPING LUMBER

SAW HORSES

#15

You can use four chairs of equal height, or four boxes. Plastic milk cartons are very handy, but even corrugated cardboard liquor boxes will do (see illus. #16). Leave the dividers in them, stand

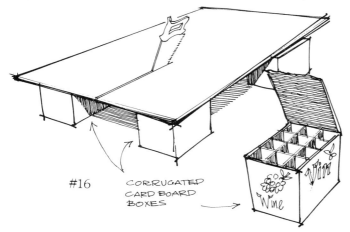

#16   CORRUGATED CARD BOARD BOXES

them upright, and position the boxes so that the plywood will not fall when it is cut through.

To start cutting, rest the saw on the far edge of the board and make several short pulls towards you. It is best to start this way because the teeth are facing slightly forward, which makes it difficult to start with a forward stroke. Make enough

backstrokes to get a good start into the wood and then push the following strokes. Keep your eye over the blade to be sure the saw is vertical. Make long even strokes, keeping your wrist as stiff as possible. Remember, only the forward stroke is doing the cutting. If you are cutting a small piece of plywood, use two clamps and clamp it to a convenient table while cutting. Even your dining-room table (protected by newspapers) can be used for this purpose. Just be sure the table underneath is not in line with the cut and that the wood is securely clamped to avoid accidentally cutting the table.

Cutting Plywood with an Electric Portable Saw
Make sure the piece you are sawing off is supported on the same level as the original piece. Place the supports under the plywood so that the pieces fall away from the cut when you finish cutting the panel (see illus. #17). Always keep a long straight piece of 1/2 x 4 in. handy for use as a guide when you want to cut long straight cuts (ripping). This is done by clamping the two ends of the straightedge to the plywood and parallel to the cut. The distance from the cut is determined

CUTTING PLYWOOD WITH AN ELECTRIC PORTABLE SAW

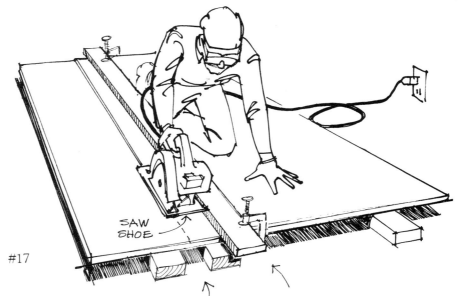

SAW SHOE

#17

PLACE SUPPORTS UNDER THE WOOD YOU ARE CUTTING SO THE PIECES FALL AWAY FROM THE CUT WHEN YOU ARE FINISHED.

CLAMP A STRAIGHTEDGE PARALLEL TO THE CUT YOU WANT TO MAKE. THE DISTANCE FROM THE CUT IS DETERMINED BY MEASURING THE DISTANCE FROM THE BLADE TO THE SIDE OF THE SHOE.

by measuring the distance from the blade to the side of the saw shoe.

Note that with any power tool you should always check before starting to see that the electric cord is behind you or off to one side so that you don't cut through it.

Drawers, Shelves, and Other Storage

Drawers

Drawers are the most difficult part of any carpentry job. Great skill is required to measure and cut them to tolerances of 1/16 in. The secret lies in making sure that the drawer and the cabinet it fits into are absolutely square in *all directions*. A professional cabinetmaker checks for squareness before, during, and after each operation.

There are four main points to consider when making a drawer:

1. Measure the space the drawer will occupy from side to side, front to back, and top to bottom.

2. You must decide if the drawer will fit inside the cabinet space or overlap the front edges of the cabinet (see illus. #18). The drawer that fits inside the cabinet must be a perfect fit, with a consistant 1/16 in. crack showing between the drawer front and the front edge of the cabinet. This can sometimes be quite difficult, especially if you have several drawers. One way to avoid this problem is to indent or recess the drawer 1/2 in. so that the drawer purposely does not line up with the front edge of the cabinet (see illus. #19). In this type of construction the face edge of the cabinet must be finished off in some special way.

Another solution is to construct drawers with a front that overlaps the front edge of the cabinet. Here again there is a problem of finishing off the side edges of the drawer, which will show (although not as much as the front). This type of drawer provides a better air seal because it overlaps and touches the front edge of the cabinet (see illus. #20).

3. If the drawer is small (under 4 in. high and 16 in. wide) it is advisable to use 1/2 in. clear pine for the sides, back, and front; if the drawer is medium size (6 in. high and 24 in. wide) it is advisable to use 1/2 in. plywood; and if the

DRAWERS
3 TYPES OF
DRAWER CONFIGURATIONS

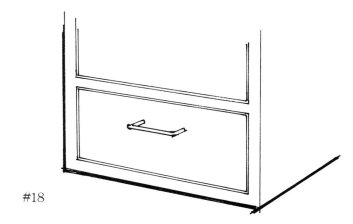

#18

DRAWER FRONT FLUSH WITH THE CABINET FRONT EDGES.

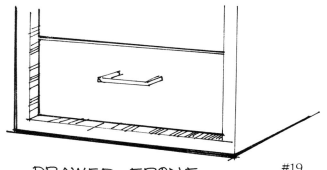

#19

DRAWER FRONT RECESSED IN FROM THE CABINET FRONT EDGES.

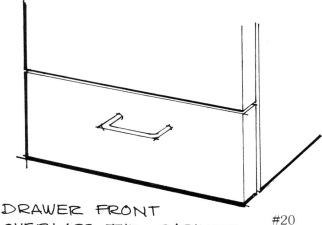

#20

DRAWER FRONT OVERLAPS THE CABINET FRONT EDGES.

drawer is much larger, use 5/8 in. or 3/4 in. plywood.

4. When planning your drawer, decide beforehand how it will be supported and by what means it will slide in and out. There are many ways to do this. The simplest is to cut a dado groove with a router or table saw into the side of each drawer from front to back and to attach a stick (cleat) the same length but slightly thinner onto the side walls of the cabinet. The drawer slides on the two runners and requires only a 1/16 in. clearance on either side of the drawer.

This type of drawer slide works well if the drawer is small and the groove can be cut in the sides through 1/2 in. soft pine with a router. If you don't have a router you can make the slide by nailing and subsequently gluing two strips of 1/4 x 3/4 in. wood onto each side of the drawer and attaching another similar strip to the inside of

the cabinet (see illus. #21 of Simple Lap Joint Drawer). Remember, you must allow at least 1/4 in. on each side between the drawer and the side of the cabinet to compensate for the extra thickness of wood, plus another 1/16 in. on each side for general clearance.

Drawers that are made with lap joints rather than professional-looking dado joints are perfectly all right as long as they are well glued. They take less time to make but will only last about fifty years, whereas the other joint will last over a century.

How to Make a Simple Lap-Joint Drawer
Here is a way to make a drawer using only a hand saw, a hammer, and a T-square.

1. Follow the first three points listed above.
2. Cut all pieces from 1/2 in. wood. Measure the cabinet opening and cut the true front *slightly* smaller than the opening.

SIMPLE LAP–JOINT DRAWER

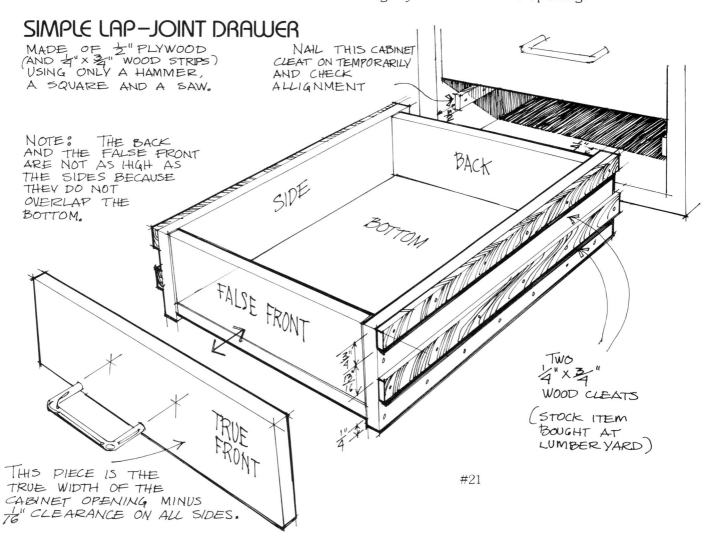

MADE OF ½" PLYWOOD (AND ¼" x ¾" WOOD STRIPS) USING ONLY A HAMMER, A SQUARE AND A SAW.

NAIL THIS CABINET CLEAT ON TEMPORARILY AND CHECK ALLIGNMENT

NOTE: THE BACK AND THE FALSE FRONT ARE NOT AS HIGH AS THE SIDES BECAUSE THEY DO NOT OVERLAP THE BOTTOM.

SIDE

BACK

BOTTOM

FALSE FRONT

TRUE FRONT

TWO ¼" x ¾" WOOD CLEATS

(STOCK ITEM BOUGHT AT LUMBER YARD)

THIS PIECE IS THE TRUE WIDTH OF THE CABINET OPENING MINUS 1/16" CLEARANCE ON ALL SIDES.

#21

3. The back and the false front are identical in size. To make them, subtract 1/2 in. from the width of the true front and 3/4 in. from the height of the true front. The sides are the same height as the true front; the length is found by measuring the depth of the cabinet opening and subtracting 1/2 in.

4. The bottom is the same width as the false front and back. The length is the same dimension as the sides minus 1/4 in.

5. The sides, false front, and back are glued and nailed to the bottom (see illus. #22). Check

HOW TO CLAMP PIECES TOGETHER WITHOUT FURNITURE CLAMPS

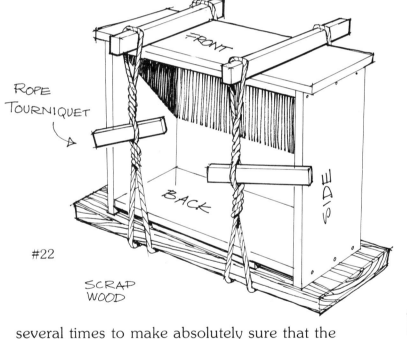

several times to make absolutely sure that the drawer is square in all directions. Take the diagonal measurement between two corners and compare it with the measurement between the other two corners. They should be exactly the same.

6. Nail the 1/2 x 3/4 in. side cleats onto the sides of the drawer using 5/8 in. brads. Do not glue, since they may need adjustments later. Make sure they are level with the top of the drawer sides, then glue.

Important: Before the glue has dried, place the drawer in the cabinet space to make sure it fits. If

it doesn't, you'll still have time to tear it apart and make adjustments.

7. When the glue has dried, carefully mark where the 1/4 x 3/4 in. cleat should go on the inside of the cabinet wall. It should be 3/4 in. below the top of the drawer. Temporarily nail it in place using 5/8 in. brads (do not glue yet!) and test the drawer to see if it slides smoothly. Chances are it won't and the slides will have to be removed and repositioned. If the nails start to go in the original holes again, take them completely out and start them in a new spot.

8. When everything is nice and square and fits just right, nail and glue the true front to the completed drawer. Use thin 2 in. long finishing nails and countersink them below the surface of the wood with a large blunt nail or a professional nail set (see illus. #23).

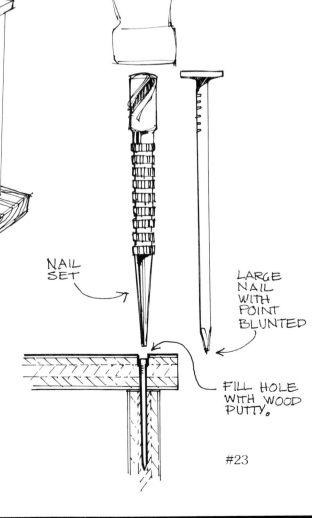

How to Make a More Professional and Longer-Lasting Drawer Using Rabbet and Dado Joints (Illus. #24)

PROFESSIONAL DRAWER
Lasts longer but requires an electric router or table saw to make it

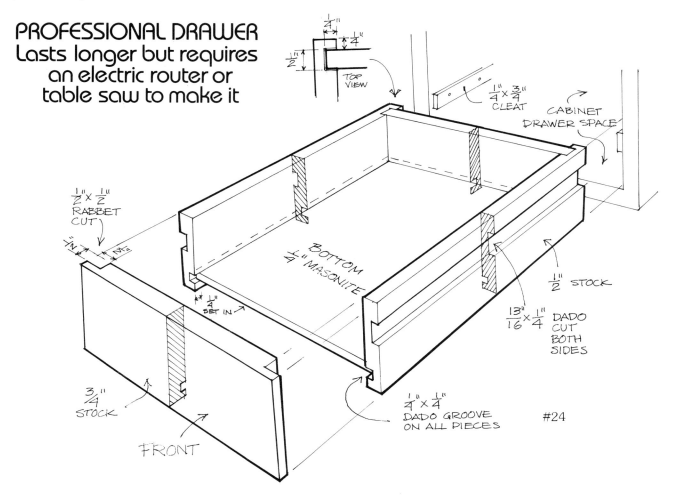

TOP VIEW

$\frac{1}{4}$"

$\frac{1}{4}$"

$\frac{1}{2}$"

$\frac{1}{4}$" × $\frac{3}{4}$" CLEAT

CABINET DRAWER SPACE

$\frac{1}{2}$" × $\frac{1}{2}$" RABBET CUT

$\frac{1}{4}$" × $\frac{1}{4}$" SET IN

BOTTOM $\frac{1}{4}$" MASONITE

$\frac{1}{2}$" STOCK

$\frac{13}{16}$" × $\frac{1}{4}$" DADO CUT BOTH SIDES

$\frac{3}{4}$" STOCK

FRONT

$\frac{1}{4}$" × $\frac{1}{4}$" DADO GROOVE ON ALL PIECES

#24

1. Follow points 1 through 4 above.

2. The two side pieces are the full depth of the cabinet opening minus 1/4 in.

3. The back piece is the width of the cabinet opening minus 1/16 in. on each side (for clearance) and minus an additional 1/2 in. (assuming you are using 1/2 in. stock).

4. The front piece is cut from 3/4 in. stock the same width as the cabinet opening (minus 1/16 in. clearance).

Be sure to label all pieces so that you know which side to cut on.

5. Using an electric router or table saw, cut a 1/4 in. wide dado (groove), 1/4 in. deep, and 1/4 in. in from the bottom edge of all the pieces. This is the groove into which the bottom panel will fit.

6. Cut a dado 13/16 in. wide along the outside of each piece and 3/4 in. from the top edge.

7. From a piece of 1/4 in. masonite cut the bot-tom panel slightly smaller than the width of the back panel. Cut the panel in the other direction long enough to fit 1/4 in. into the back and front pieces.

8. Make a 1/4 in. deep dado cut (as shown in illus. #24), 1/4 in. from the back end to accept the back piece.

9. Make a 1/2 in. wide rabbet cut, 1/4 in. deep, into the two back ends of the front piece in order to accept the sides.

10. Assemble the drawer without glue or nails, placing it in the cabinet space to see if all the pieces fit together correctly. Then glue and nail the pieces together and place them in the cabinet for a final check before the glue hardens.

11. Cut two pieces of 1/4 x 3/4 in. wood strips, making them 1/4 in. shorter than the depth of the cabinet drawer space. Nail them onto each side of the cabinet walls, placing them 3/4 in. down

from the top. Make sure they are parallel and even. Test to see if the drawer slides smoothly. If it doesn't fit perfectly, adjust the side cleats, finally gluing and nailing them permanently in place.

Drawer Slides
Many professional carpenters insist that metal telescoping ball-bearing slides are the only way to hang a drawer. Indeed they do pull smoothly and can be adjusted easily, but they are also expensive.

If you plan to use metal slides, leave 1/2 in. clearance on either side of the drawer as in illus. #25, omitting the dado groove and cleats. Fol-

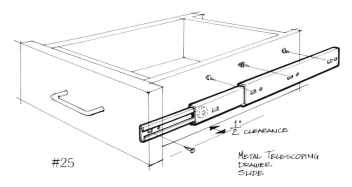

#25

METAL TELESCOPING
DRAWER
SLIDE

low the mounting directions on the package and screw the corresponding sections onto the side of the drawer and the inside of the cabinet, using the slotted holes. When you are sure the drawer fits properly, use the round holes to screw it permanently in place.

Shelves

Probably the most necessary item in any child's room, regardless of his or her age, is additional shelf space for toys, games, art supplies, etc. You should decide early on whether this storage should be left open to view or enclosed behind drawers or doors.

People tend to build shelves more than anything else, probably because shelves appear so simple to construct. And they are easy to build as long as you follow a few basic rules:

1. Make plans on paper and double-check measurements.

2. Don't make shelves span more than 3 feet without a support or they will bend in the middle under a heavy load (especially records). Exception: If you are using 5/4 in. wood, which is

thicker, stronger, and better looking than 3/4 in. stock, you can allow up to 4-foot spans.

3. If you plan to have shelves go against a wall, be aware of the baseboard at floor level and notch out the wood to allow for this.

4. Floors are rarely perfectly flat, so check with a level and trim off the bottom of the shelf where necessary.

5. If the shelves you are making go higher than 3 feet, attach them to the wall so they cannot be pulled over accidentally.

6. If you are renting an apartment and plan to move in the near future, choose a design that you can disassemble and take with you when you leave.

7. Wood: #2 common 1 x 12 in. lumber is acceptable if you plan on painting the shelves when you are finished. It saves time if you give all the lumber a prime coat using a roller before assembling. The knots in #2 common lumber can bleed through the paint if you don't seal them with a good shellac-base sealer first.

The best wood to buy is 5/4 in. clear white pine — if you don't mind how very expensive it is.

Another alternative to #2 common pine, if you like a rustic look, is common 2 x 8 in. or 2 x 10 in. thick construction lumber. This lumber is actually 1-1/2 in. thick and can take heavy loads. If stained a dark brown or even ebony it can look quite handsome. This type of lumber requires too much sanding to make it suitable for painting, so don't consider using it if your child's room decor is light and delicate.

The simplest (but not the cheapest) shelves are 1 x 10 in. boards supported on metal brackets that are in turn attached to metal vertical standards (see illus. #26). These are screwed to the

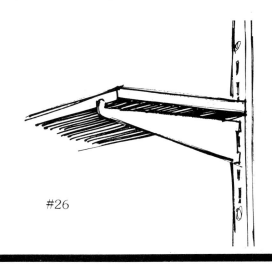

#26

17

wall with 1-1/2 in. long flathead screws. Be sure to level the standards to the same height on the wall. The only problem with this system is that there is nothing at the ends of the shelf to keep objects from falling off.

The second simplest — and the cheapest — method of construction is the open standing shelf shown (illus. #27), which gives the objects to be

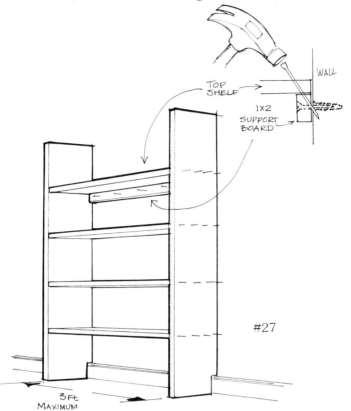

#27

stored a more enclosed look. The pieces can all be precut at your lumberyard for an additional charge, so all you need to do is sand the lumber and nail it together. You can vary the number of shelves to suit your needs, but if you make shelves tall like these, be sure and attach them to the walls as shown in illus. #27. This will also keep the shelves from racking (moving out of square).

How to Make Open Shelves

1. Measure the space you want the shelves to fit into and check the floor to make sure it's level and at right angles to the wall.

2. Draw a plan on a piece of paper indicating the height of the shelves. The depth is determined by the dimension of the boards you use. Most 3/4 in. thick lumber (referred to as 1 in.

thick lumber by the lumberyard) comes in the following:

1 x 2 but actually is 3/4 x 1-1/2
1 x 3 but actually is 3/4 x 2-1/2
1 x 4 but actually is 3/4 x 3-1/2
1 x 6 but actually is 3/4 x 5-1/2
1 x 8 but actually is 3/4 x 7-1/4
1 x 10 but actually is 3/4 x 9-1/4
1 x 12 but actually is 3/4 x 11-1/4

Note: make sure when selecting the wide boards (1 x 10 in. and 1 x 12 in.) to avoid cupped or warped boards.

3. You can have your shelves cut out of a 4 x 8 ft. sheet of plywood, which will make it slightly stronger, but you must cover the edges with wooden strips to make it look finished. This can be done in two ways:

Either nail a 3/4 x 1/4 in. clear pine wood strip onto the front edge of the shelf using finishing nails; set the nails in and fill with plastic wood (illus. #28).

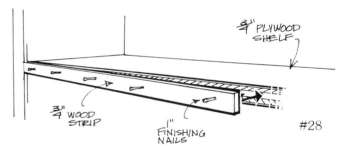

#28

Or cover it with wood tape sold at lumberyards (illus. #29).

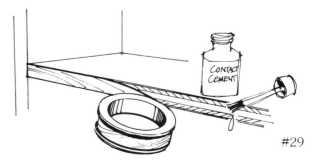

#29

4. Order the wood precut at the lumberyard. Give the cutter a cutting plan if you are using plywood. (Remember, you pay for the whole piece of plywood, so make sure you get the scrap pieces with your order; they can come in handy for other projects.)

The advantage of ordering wood precut is that you can pick out the individual pieces yourself and bring them right home, all cut to size and ready to assemble.

5. If not precut, cut the wood to the desired lengths and lay them on the floor in your child's room. If necessary, sand the wood and prefinish it while it is still unassembled. Fill any holes or knots with plastic wood or water-base wood putty and sand smooth.

6. Lay the two upright sides down on the floor next to each other with the good edge on the outside and mark two lines with a T-square where the shelves will go, marking across both boards at the same time (see illus. #30).

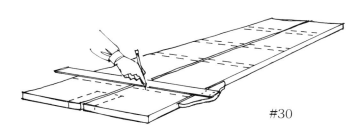

#30

7. Notch out the back lower edge to accept the baseboard (see illus #31); if necessary, trim off the bottom to conform to the irregularities of the floor.

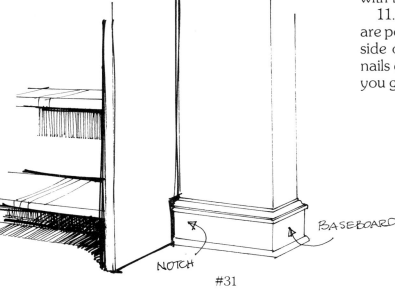

BASEBOARD

NOTCH

#31

8. Turn the boards over and mark with a light dashed line the *center* where the shelves will be positioned on the reverse side (see illus #32). This will be your guide for your nails. Now nail 10d (3 in.) nails at 3 in. intervals across the board so that their points are just protruding through to the other side.

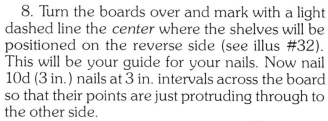

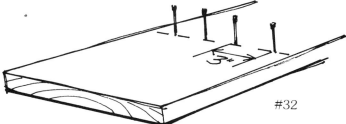

#32

9. When you have started all the nails, turn the board up on its long edge. Position it at right angles to the wall and wedge two of the shelves between the wall and the side board to support it while nailing (see illus #33).

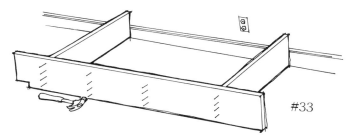

#33

10. Make sure the shelves are in their proper position between the pencil lines you drew (see Step 6 above) and hammer the nails. Repeat with the other shelves until all are completed.

11. Turn the structure over so that the shelves are pointing up and carefully position the second side over the ends of the shelves. Hammer the nails completely through, checking alignment as you go along (see illus. #34).

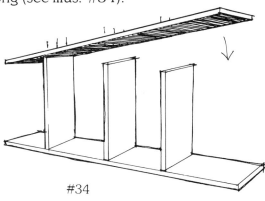

#34

12. Stand the structure up, moving it into position so it is resting against the wall. Don't be upset by how weak it feels, as this will be corrected in the final step.

Carefully measure and cut a 1 x 2 in. support board, nailing it to the wall directly under the top shelf. Then nail one 3 in. finishing nail every foot along the top shelf at an angle, so that the nail penetrates the support board. This will make the shelf semipermanently attached to the wall and safe for your child (see illus. #27).

Other Storage

There may come a time when you feel you've lost the battle of orderliness in your child's room. Don't despair. After all, you're the one in charge here — aren't you?

It is a good idea at some point to view the child's room in relation to the objects it will hold, their shapes, and their accessibility. You can do this by taking a pad and pencil and systematically going around your child's room jotting down every object you see, right down to the last stub of crayon. List each item by name, shape, and the type of storage it's best suited to. A random check of my own child's room revealed the following:

Item	Shape	Type of Storage Required
Record player	low box	table top
records	flat, 12 in. square	vertical on shelf
books	flat, 13 in. (largest)	vertical on shelf
puzzles	flat	horizontal on shelf
blocks	vary from 3 to 8 in. long	box on wheels
dolls	vary from 5 to 14 in. tall	display on high shelf
Fisher Price House	14 x 16 x 10 in.	box on wheels
cash register	8 x 10 x 9 in.	shelf near floor
bank	3 x 4 x 5 in.	shelf (high)
car-park toy	14 x 18 x 14 in.	floor
tinker toys	cylinder 5 in. diameter x 14 in.	shelf (high)
puzzles	flat, 12 x 12 in.	medium-high shelf
Lego	large flat box, 20 x 14 in.	low shelf
Crystal Climbers	flat box 14 x 12 in.	low shelf
Richard Scarry Medical Center	flat box 16 x 14 in.	low shelf
plastic toy clock	10 x 10 in.	high shelf
balls and tops	vary	low box
costumes	18 x 30 in.	suitcase or foot locker
hats	vary	pegs
marbles	small bag	small pull-out compartment
stickers	flat envelope	small pull-out compartment
art supplies	large box	table top
sports equipment		in closet
bicycle		floor space

As you can see from the above list, the problem of where to store what and how can be solved by building a few strategic storage units. One may scoff at grandma's adage "a place for everything and everything in its place," but it does make life easier, not only for the parent, but for the child as well. Children can be taught to enjoy putting things in their proper place when doing so is approached as a game. And building storage for your child's things can be approached in the same spirit.

MISCELLANEOUS SHELF HINTS

← OPEN SHELVES
MADE FROM 2"x12"
CONSTRUCTION LUMBER

TO INCREASE THE STRENGTH,
CUT DADO GROOVES IN THE
END BOARDS AND SET THE
SHELVES IN $\frac{1}{4}$". BESIDES
PROVIDING A REST FOR THE
SHELF, THE DADO GROOVE
ALLOWS FOR A GREATER
GLUING AREA FOR THE JOINT.

CUT DADO GROOVES WITH A
DADO SAW.

#35

STAIN THE SHELVES DARK
TO HIDE THE IMPERFECTIONS
OF THE ROUGH LUMBER.

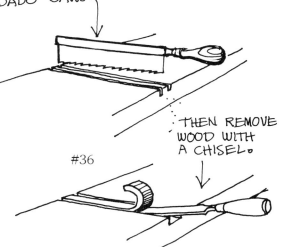

#36

THEN REMOVE
WOOD WITH
A CHISEL.

OPEN SHELVES CAN BE
MADE FREE-STANDING,
SIMILAR TO A ROOM
DIVIDER, BY SECURING
THE UPRIGHT TO THE CEILING.

TWO WAYS TO ATTACH THE UPRIGHTS TO THE CEILING

1.

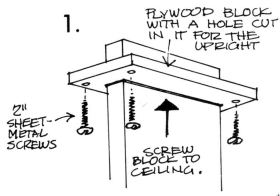

PLYWOOD BLOCK
WITH A HOLE CUT
IN IT FOR THE
UPRIGHT

1"
SHEET-
METAL
SCREWS

SCREW
BLOCK TO
CEILING.

#37

2.

$\frac{3}{8}$"x 3" CARRIAGE
BOLTS

NUT RECESSED
AND GLUED INTO
TOP END OF UPRIGHT

⊛ CUT UPRIGHTS 1" SHORTER
THAN CEILING HEIGHT.

○ THREAD CARRIAGE BOLTS INTO
RECESSED NUTS.

○ RAISE SHELVES AND UNSCREW
BOLTS UNTIL THEY TOUCH CEILING.

SINGLE SHELVES

SOMETIMES IT IS NICE TO
HAVE A SINGLE SHELF
JUST WHERE YOU NEED IT.
A SINGLE SHELF MUST BE
SELF-SUPPORTING AND SECURELY
ATTACHED TO THE WALL.
HERE ARE SOME SOLUTIONS.

THIS RUSTIC SHELF...

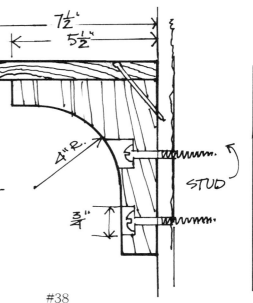

... REQUIRES NO
TRIPS TO THE HARDWARE
STORE.

    THE WOODEN BRACKETS ARE CUT
WITH A SABER SAW FROM A 2×6.
CENTER THE BRACKETS 16" APART
AND SCREW THEM THROUGH THE WALL
INTO THE STUDS.

#38

METAL SHELF BRACKETS

METAL BRACKETS
ARE AVAILABLE AT
HARDWARE STORES
IN MANY SIZES.

IF THE SHELF IS INTENDED TO SUPPORT
HEAVY OBJECTS, YOU MUST USE LEAD OR PLASTIC
ANCHORS IN PLASTER WALLS.
NOTE: IT IS IMPORTANT TO DRILL THE CORRECT
SIZE HOLE FOR THESE ANCHORS. — ASK YOUR
HARDWARE SALESMAN FOR THE RIGHT DRILL.

COMBINATION SHELF
AND CLOTHES RACK

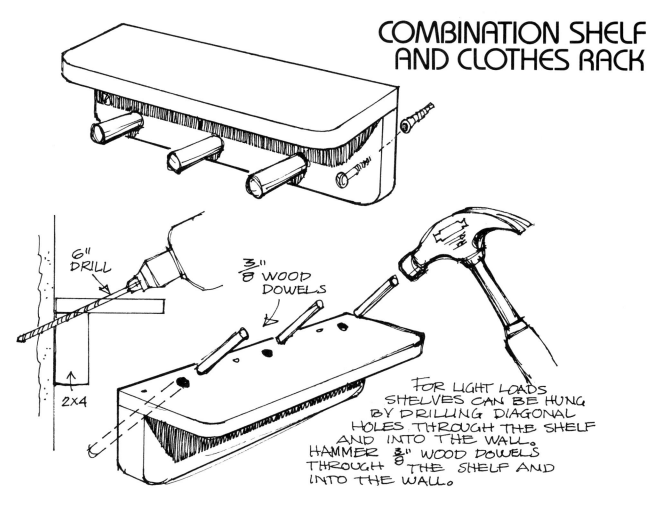

6" DRILL

$\frac{3}{8}$" WOOD DOWELS

2x4

FOR LIGHT LOADS
SHELVES CAN BE HUNG
BY DRILLING DIAGONAL
HOLES THROUGH THE SHELF
AND INTO THE WALL.
HAMMER $\frac{3}{8}$" WOOD DOWELS
THROUGH THE SHELF AND
INTO THE WALL.

#39

SECTION 2: FIFTEEN PROJECTS

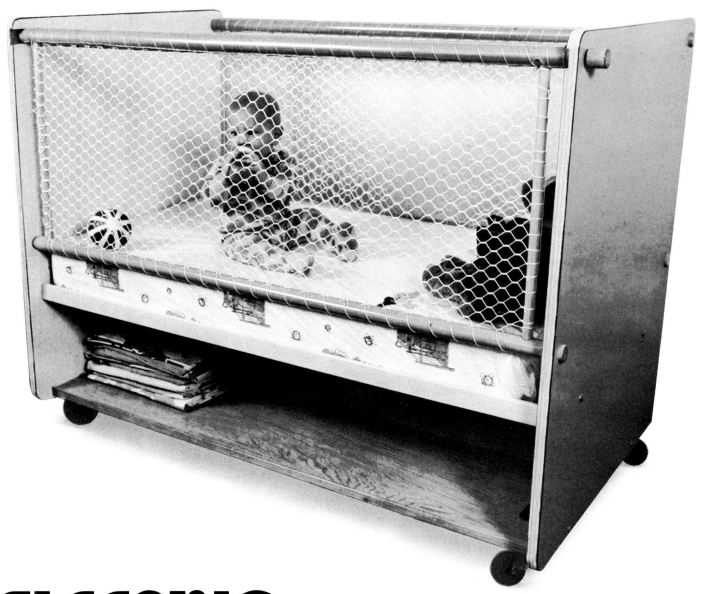

CRIB

All cribs must be assembled in the child's room since the standard crib is too wide to fit through most door openings. This crib was designed to be assembled and disassembled easily without complicated directions or tools.

The front can be unlocked and swung down out of the way when changing the bed sheets.

The top rails are protected by two pieces of 1-3/8 in. diameter clear vinyl tubing, which can be bought at plastic stores or through boat hardware suppliers. Vinyl is extremely safe and, since it's nontoxic, provides an excellent surface for the baby to teethe on.

This crib uses a standard 27-1/4 x 52 x 5-1/2 in. crib mattress available at any baby supply store. It has a shelf underneath for diapers, blankets, etc. and a shelf in the back for storage of out-of-season clothes. It has a soft nylon rope netting instead of the rigid bars found on most conventional cribs, and the top can be converted into a couch or seat after the child outgrows the storage-crib.

If you've ever been confronted with the problem of assembling a standard child's crib — consisting of metal rods, small springs, brackets, and screws — you'll appreciate the simplicity of this design. It's essentially composed of two plywood panels, a flat support panel, a center divider for added strength, a shelf, and four poles.

To make the crib, cut out two panels of 3/4 in. A/D plywood 43 x 32 in. and glue plastic laminate to both faces. Round off the corners and edges (see illus. #13 on page 9). Cut the holes for the 1-3/8 in. diameter rails as shown in illus. #41 with a hole saw. Cut the dado grooves as shown in the side-view section on illus. #42. Although using an electric router is the quickest method, it can also be done with a simple carbide knife, a hammer, and a chisel (see illus. #58, page 42). It will take you about two hours on each panel to complete this task. Drill the 3/8 in. bolt hole as shown.

The support, divider, and shelf panels are all 53-1/2 in. long, allowing 1/4 in. to fit into the dado grooves on each side. Cut a 3/4 in. wide dado groove 1/4 in. deep down the

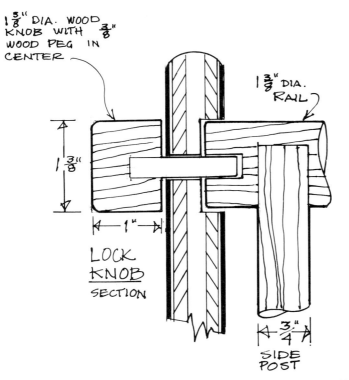

1 3/8" DIA. WOOD KNOB WITH 3/8" WOOD PEG IN CENTER

1 3/8" DIA. RAIL

1 3/8"

1"

LOCK KNOB SECTION

3/4"

SIDE POST

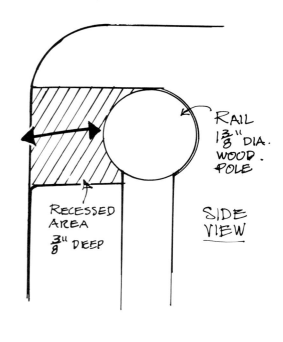

RAIL 1 3/8" DIA. WOOD POLE

RECESSED AREA 3/8" DEEP

SIDE VIEW

#41

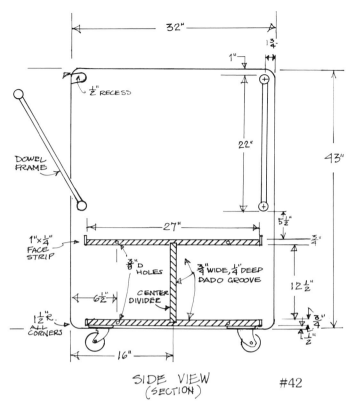

32"

1¾"

1"

½" RECESS

DOWEL FRAME

22"

43"

27"

5½"

¾"

1"x¼" FACE STRIP

⅜"D HOLES

¾" WIDE, ¼" DEEP DADO GROOVE

12½"

6½"

CENTER DIVIDER

1½"R. ALL CORNERS

¾"

½"

16"

SIDE VIEW
(SECTION)

#42

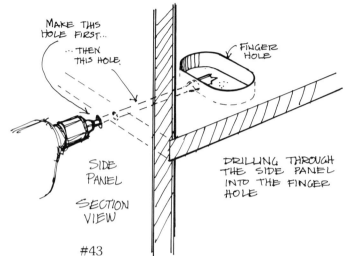

MAKE THIS HOLE FIRST...

...THEN THIS HOLE.

FINGER HOLE

SIDE PANEL

SECTION VIEW

#43

DRILLING THROUGH THE SIDE PANEL INTO THE FINGER HOLE

center of the support panel and the shelf panel. The divider is cut 13 in. high, allowing 1/4 in. to fit into the support above and the shelf below. Test the pieces to see that they fit easily into their prospective grooves.

As mentioned earlier, the crib can be assembled and disassembled easily. This is because all the fastening is done with bolts and wing nuts. Cut-out holes or finger holes must be made to allow a space for the fingers to turn the wing nuts. This can be done with the same 1-3/8 in. hole saw you use for the rail holes.

To make the bolt holes align properly, hold the horizontal and side panel pieces together and place a mark where the bolt holes should go. Using a 3/8 in. spade drill, start the hole from the inside of the side panel. As you see the point begin to come through the other side, stop and finish the hole from the other side. Then position the two pieces together again. Drill through the hole in the side panel and into the edge of the adjoining plywood until you come all the way through into the finger hole.

Drill slowly, frequently checking to see that the drill is straight (see illus. #43 and #44). An oversize, 3/8 in. hole is made in

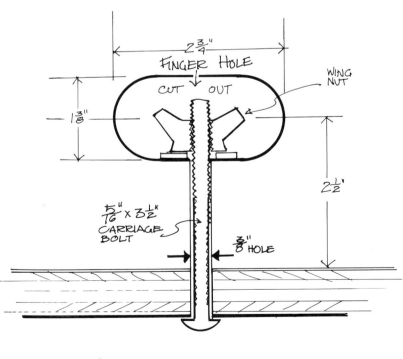

2¾"

FINGER HOLE

CUT OUT

WING NUT

1⅜"

2½"

5/16" X 3½" CARRIAGE BOLT

⅜" HOLE

FASTENING DETAIL

#44

CRIB

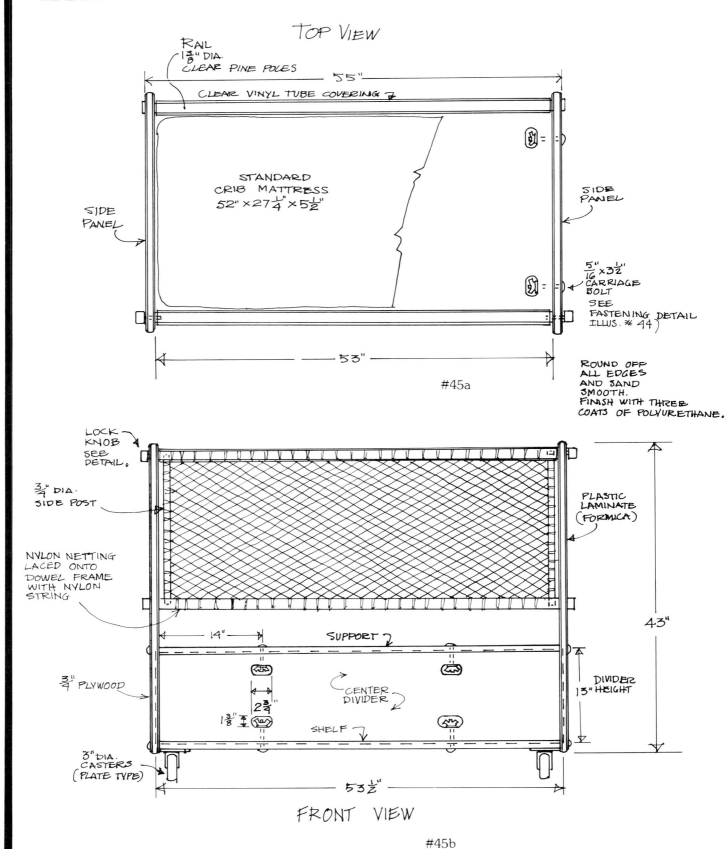

TOP VIEW

RAIL
1 3/8" DIA.
CLEAR PINE POLES

55"

CLEAR VINYL TUBE COVERING

STANDARD
CRIB MATTRESS
52" × 27 1/4" × 5 1/2"

SIDE
PANEL

SIDE
PANEL

SIDE
PANEL

5/16" × 3 1/2"
CARRIAGE
BOLT

SEE
FASTENING DETAIL
ILLUS. # 44)

53"

#45a

ROUND OFF
ALL EDGES
AND SAND
SMOOTH.
FINISH WITH THREE
COATS OF POLYURETHANE.

LOCK
KNOB
SEE
DETAIL.

3/4" DIA.
SIDE POST

PLASTIC
LAMINATE
(FORMICA)

NYLON NETTING
LACED ONTO
DOWEL FRAME
WITH NYLON
STRING

43"

14"

SUPPORT

3/4" PLYWOOD

CENTER
DIVIDER

DIVIDER
13" HEIGHT

2 3/4"

1 3/8"

SHELF

3" DIA.
CASTERS
(PLATE TYPE)

53 1/2"

FRONT VIEW

#45b

case of slight variations in final alignment. Follow this same procedure for all finger holes.

The lock knob is a safety catch and holds the top front rail in place. It's made by boring a 3/8 in. diameter hole in the center of a 1-3/8 in. diameter knob and a similar hole through the side panel and into the center of the top rail (see illus. #41). A 3/8 in. diameter peg 1-1/2 in. long is glued into the knob. To unlock the top front rail, the knobs are pulled partially out on both sides and the frame is swung down.

Sand all edges smooth, using wood filler where needed, and give all surfaces (except the plastic laminate) three coats of polyurethane (see illus. #45a). Note: Use Varathane R Clear Liquid Plastic made by Flecto —recommended for use on children's furniture. Being concerned by the warning on the label that the product contained "petroleum distillates...harmful if taken internally," I wrote to the Flecto Company. Their answer in part was that "Varathane may be used with confidence on children's toys or furniture as the dry film is nontoxic.... The petroleum distillates ... evaporate as the coating dries."

Lace the netting onto the rails using white nylon string. The protective vinyl tubing is cut along the underside (with scissors), opened up, and snapped over the top rails (see illus. #45b). It stays in place of its own accord and can be snapped off if necessary.

If you've followed all of these instructions, congratulations! You are now the proud owner of a well-made crib that won't rust or mar, is easy to clean, is safe for children, is easy to move, and can be passed on from generation to generation.

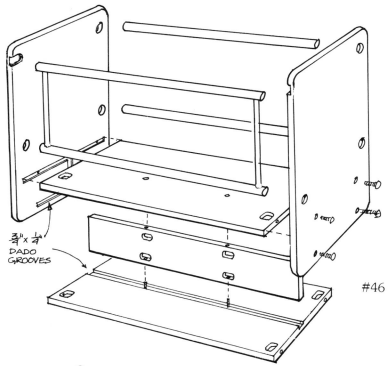

3/4" x 1/4"
DADO
GROOVES

#46

Crib Becomes a Couch

When the child outgrows the crib, it can be easily changed into a couch with storage underneath. It also doubles as an extra bed for small friends who come to stay overnight (see illus. #47 and #48). Simply cut down the two ends with a saber saw and add a back panel to give support to the two new bolsters. Cover the crib mattress and bolsters in an attractive fabric.

CRIB

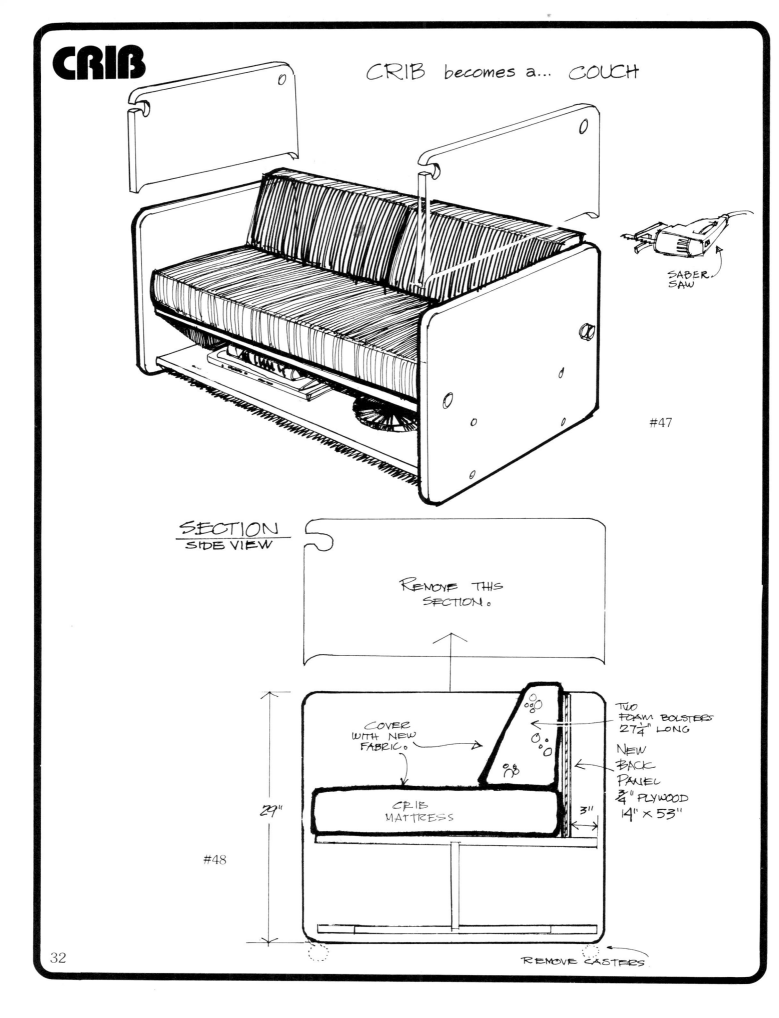

SABER
SAW

#47

SECTION
SIDE VIEW

REMOVE THIS
SECTION.

COVER
WITH NEW
FABRIC.

TWO
FOAM BOLSTERS
$27\frac{1}{4}$" LONG

NEW
BACK
PANEL
$\frac{3}{4}$" PLYWOOD
14" $\times 53$"

CRIB
MATTRESS

29"

3"

#48

REMOVE CASTERS

CHILD'S BED

CHILD'S BED

When your baby has outgrown a crib (generally around age 4) you are faced with the problem of what size bed to invest in next. You could buy a youth bed, which measures 33 x 66 in., but you might end up making your own sheets to fit it. A wiser solution is to allow your child to sleep in the crib a few more months and then make the jump to a standard size twin bed, which measures 39 x 75 in. This way you'll always find sheets and blankets to fit it. You may want to put a pillow under the edge of the mattress to slope it slightly upward, or place a chair next to it until your child gets used to having no sides on the bed. One last tip: buy the mattress before you make the bed and check the measurements to be sure they are actually 39 x 75 in.

PROCEDURE FOR SCREWING THE
SIDE AND END BOARDS TO THE LEGS

1. MARK THE EXACT LOCATION FOR EACH SCREW.

2. DRILL A $\frac{1}{2}$" DIAMETER HOLE $\frac{1}{4}$" DEEP.

3. DRILL A HOLE THE SAME SIZE OR SLIGHTLY LARGER THROUGH THE BOARD.

4. DRILL A HOLE SLIGHTLY SMALLER INTO THE LEG (PILOT HOLE).

5. SCREW A $1\frac{1}{2}$" #10 FLATHEAD SCREW INTO THE HOLE.

6. FILL THE REMAINING $\frac{1}{2}$" DIAMETER HOLE WITH A WOOD DOWEL OR WOOD FILLER.

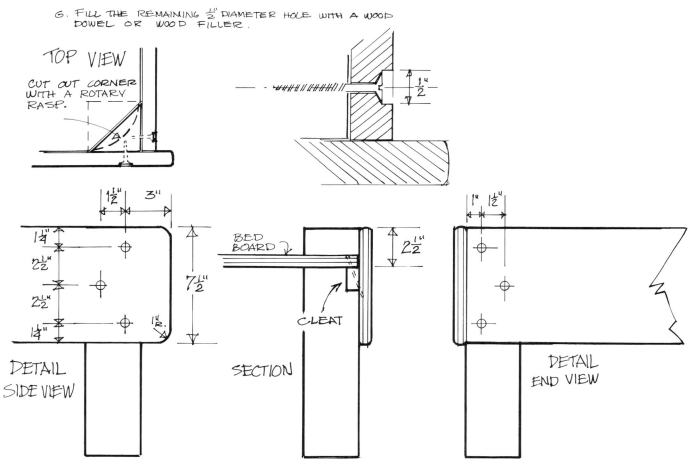

TOP VIEW

CUT OUT CORNER WITH A ROTARY RASP.

BED BOARD

CLEAT

DETAIL SIDE VIEW

SECTION

DETAIL END VIEW

#49a

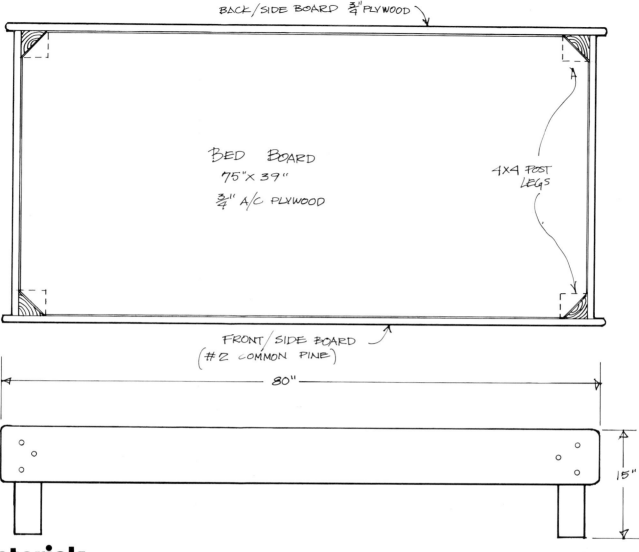

BACK/SIDE BOARD 3/4" PLYWOOD

BED BOARD
75" X 39"
3/4" A/C PLYWOOD

4X4 POST LEGS

A

FRONT/SIDE BOARD
(#2 COMMON PINE)

80"

15"

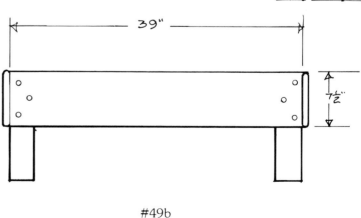

39"

7½"

#49b

Materials

The child's bed can *almost* be made from one piece of 3/4 in. plywood ($23 at the time of this writing). In addition to the sheet of plywood, you need to buy one 8 ft. piece of 1 x 8. Pick this out yourself from the stack of 1 x 8 common lumber at your lumberyard. Since this side is going to show, try to find a piece that has as few knots as possible. If, however, you are going to cover this side with plastic laminate, you needn't be so particular. Make sure the wood is straight — not warped — and clean. If necessary, take it out of the storage shed and examine it in daylight before accepting it. Don't buy clear lumber unless you're willing to pay three times as much for it. A small board of clear pine can cost the same as a good bottle of French champagne!

You will also need to buy a 4 x 4 in. post. You only need 5 ft., but the lumberyard will probably require you to buy a full 6 or 8 ft. piece.

35

CHILD'S BED

How to Make the Child's Bed

Have the lumberyard cut up the piece of A/D plywood according to the cutting plan provided (see illus. #50). Cut the front/side board (from the piece of 1 x 8 you picked out) 80 in. long. Check the ends first: they may not be square and they may have marks on them. If this is the case, cut off an inch and mark 80 in. from this point on. Make sure the two end boards are *exactly* the same length as the width of the bed board (39 in.). Cut triangular notches out of each corner of the bed board to accept the feet.

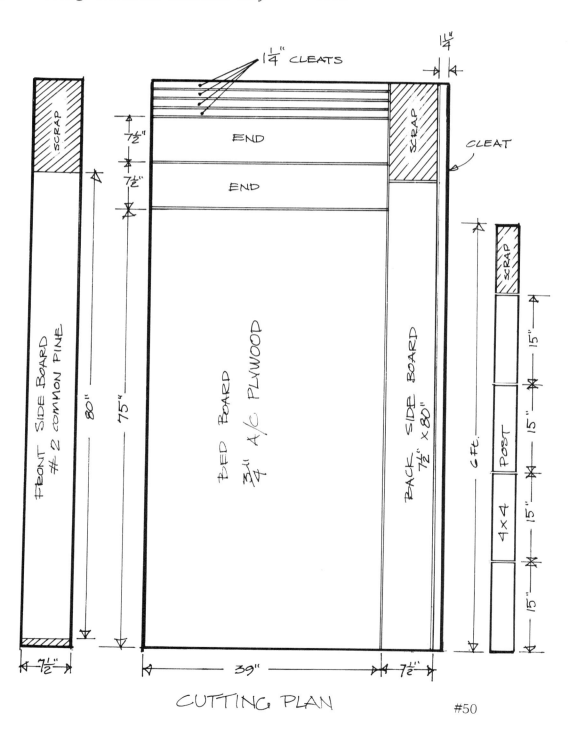

CUTTING PLAN

#50

Cut the 4 x 4 posts into 15 in. lengths. Cut a triangular piece out of the top of each piece (see illus. #51).

Lay the side boards and end boards flat on the floor with the side that will finally be next to the mattress lying face up. Measure 2-1/2 in. down from the top (see illus. #52) and glue/nail the cleat strips in place. Round off the corners of the front side

boards with a jigsaw and sand edges round (see illus. #13).

Place the 15 in. posts on the floor 75 in. apart and lay one of the side boards over them. Screw the side board onto the two feet using 1-1/2 in. flathead screws. Be sure to drill pilot holes for the screws first. Repeat the same step for the other side.

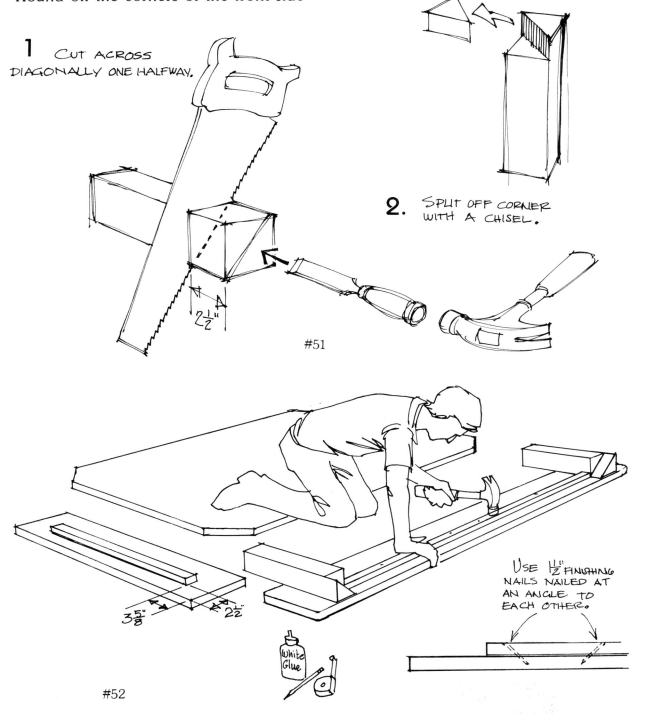

1 CUT ACROSS DIAGONALLY ONE HALFWAY.

2. SPLIT OFF CORNER WITH A CHISEL.

#51

USE 1½" FINISHING NAILS NAILED AT AN ANGLE TO EACH OTHER.

#52

CHILD'S BED

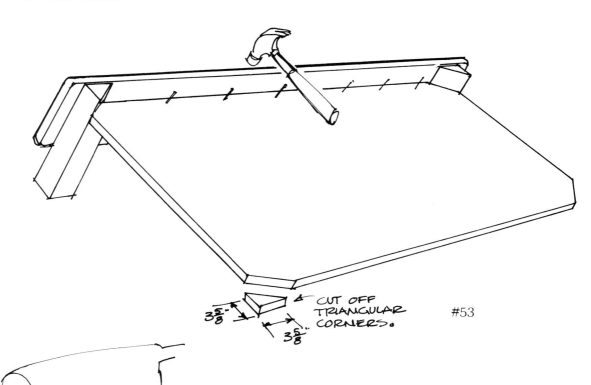

3⅝" 3⅝"

CUT OFF TRIANGULAR CORNERS.

#53

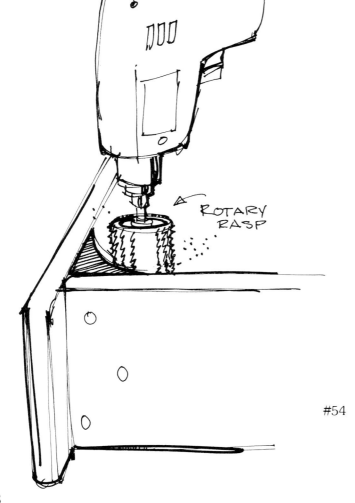

ROTARY RASP

Prop one of the side boards up and place the edge of the bed board on the cleat. Nail the bed board onto the cleat (see illus. #53), leaving the nail heads protruding 1/2 in. in case something goes wrong. Do the same for the other side and the two ends.

When the bed is completely assembled, check to see that all joints fit properly, then hammer the nails all the way in.

Set your mattress on the bed and see how it fits. If the corners are too tight, carve out an inside curve with a rotary rasp using an electric drill (see illus. #54).

#54

LOFT BED

LOFT BED

By the time your child reaches the age of eight, you may have found that the amount of available free space in his or her room is diminishing as toys, games, bikes, and sleds start to take over. One of the best ways to improve this situation, as well as to create an exciting and welcome change for your child, is to build a loft bed. This creates an entirely new space in your child's room which can be put to use as a living/play/work environment. This is also a good solution if you are having a second child share the same room: each child has his or her own special place.

The loft bed is greatly appreciated by the child, who can fantasize it as a tree house, a puppet theater, a Junglegym, or just a place to lie down and read a book.

To avoid making the bed every day (which can be difficult while perching on a ladder), we use a nylon sleeping bag on top of one contour bed sheet. Every week or so the sleeping bag gets yanked off the bed and run through the washer/dryer.

and make a wood plug with a hole in it as shown. Screw these directly to the floor. The loft bed does not require the support of the wall, so you can install it anywhere in the room. Make four 8 x 8 in. brackets for the top of each post and cut a square hole in the center so they fit loosely over the posts.

Carefully measure the distance from the floor to the ceiling for each post and cut the posts 3/8 in. shorter. This discrepancy will be hidden by the plywood bracket when it is fastened to the ceiling.

Assemble the two back posts, side board, and end boards using four 6 in. long carriage bolts. Don't tighten them until the whole structure is in place.

Align the back posts over the plugs on the floor and raise the section until it's vertical. Have someone hold it there while you go on to the next step (see illus. #57).

Assemble the two front posts and side board and raise them to meet the section already standing. Bolt all the pieces

Materials

Wood

Quantity	Description	Size (in inches) Thickness L.W.H.	Name & Location
1 pc.	A/D plywood	3/4 x 76 x 40	bed bottom
4 pcs.	posts	4 x 4 x 120	corner posts
2 pcs.	A/D plywood	3/4 x 12 x 90	side boards
2 pcs.	A/D plywood	3/4 x 12 x 40	end boards
2 pcs.	clear pine	5/4 x 9 x 79	stair sides
6 pcs.	clear pine	5/4 x 6 x 16	stair treads
1 pc.	A/D plywood	3/4 x 15 x 96	slide
2 pcs.	A/D plywood	3/4 x 4 x 66	slide sides

Hardware

1	hole saw	1-1/2	
3	angle aluminum	1 x 1 x 96	bed-board support
8	carriage bolts	3/8 x 6	post bolts
32	screw eyes	1	rope barricade
1 roll	nylon rope	3/8 x 100 ft.	rope barricade
4	carriage bolts	3/8 x 3	rope post
8	carriage bolts	3/8 x 6	corner bolts

Locate the exact position for each post on the floor and mark the floor with an X. Cut a 1-3/4 in. hole out of the bottom of each post

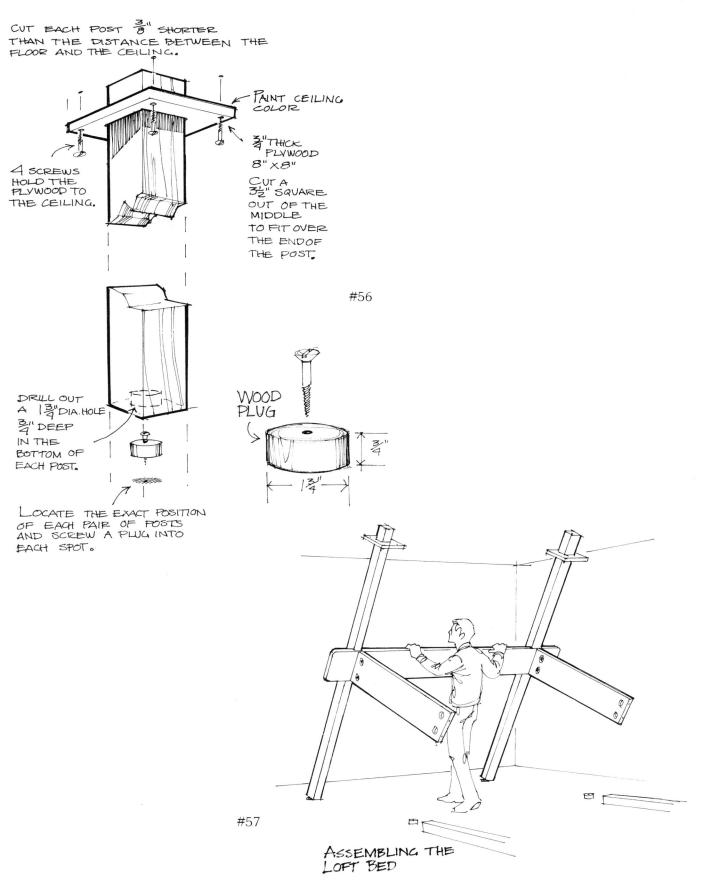

CUT EACH POST $\frac{3}{8}$" SHORTER THAN THE DISTANCE BETWEEN THE FLOOR AND THE CEILING.

PAINT CEILING COLOR

$\frac{3}{4}$" THICK PLYWOOD 8" X 8"

CUT A $3\frac{1}{2}$" SQUARE OUT OF THE MIDDLE TO FIT OVER THE END OF THE POST.

4 SCREWS HOLD THE PLYWOOD TO THE CEILING.

#56

DRILL OUT A $1\frac{3}{4}$" DIA. HOLE $\frac{3}{4}$" DEEP IN THE BOTTOM OF EACH POST.

WOOD PLUG

$\frac{3}{4}$"

$1\frac{3}{4}$"

LOCATE THE EXACT POSITION OF EACH PAIR OF POSTS AND SCREW A PLUG INTO EACH SPOT.

#57

ASSEMBLING THE LOFT BED

LOFT BED

TO MAKE A DADO GROOVE BY HAND

1. USING A CARBIDE KNIFE, MAKE REPEATED STROKES UNTIL THE PLASTIC LAMINATE IS ALMOST CUT THROUGH. THEN CHISEL IT OUT.

2. USING A UTILITY KNIFE, MAKE TWO $\frac{1}{8}$" DEEP CUTS.

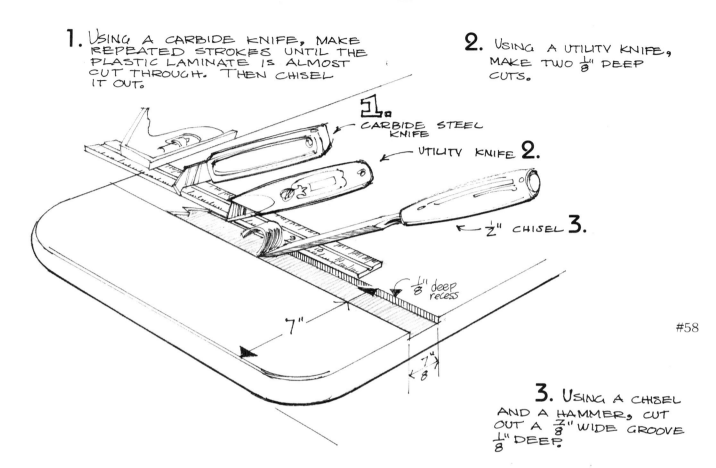

CARBIDE STEEL KNIFE

UTILITY KNIFE **2.**

$\frac{1}{2}$" CHISEL **3.**

$\frac{1}{8}$" deep recess

7"

$\frac{7}{8}$"

#58

3. USING A CHISEL AND A HAMMER, CUT OUT A $\frac{7}{8}$" WIDE GROOVE $\frac{1}{8}$" DEEP.

CORNER DETAIL

THIS TYPE OF JOINT IS GENERALLY FOUND ON HEAVY-DUTY TYPE CONSTRUCTION SUCH AS WORKBENCHES AND LOOMS. AS YOU CAN SEE, ONLY TWO BOLTS ARE NEEDED TO JOIN THE THREE PIECES TOGETHER. THESE TWO BOLTS MAKE A VERY STRONG JOINT AND AT THE SAME TIME ALLOW THE BED TO BE DISMANTLED AT A LATER DATE IN CASE YOU HAVE TO MOVE.

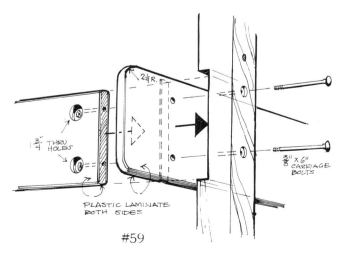

$2\frac{1}{4}$ R.

$\frac{3}{4}$" THRU HOLES

$\frac{3}{8}$" X 6" CARRIAGE BOLTS

PLASTIC LAMINATE BOTH SIDES

#59

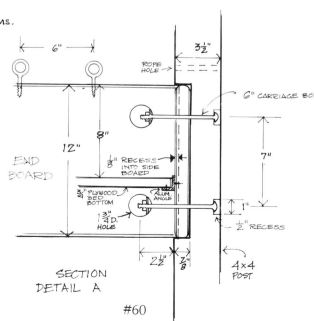

6"

ROPE HOLE

$3\frac{1}{2}$"

6" CARRIAGE BO

8"

12"

END BOARD

$\frac{1}{8}$" RECESS INTO SIDE BOARD

7"

$\frac{3}{4}$" PLYWOOD BED BOTTOM

ALUM. ANGLE

$1\frac{3}{4}$" D. HOLE

1"

$\frac{1}{2}$" RECESS

$2\frac{1}{2}$"

$\frac{7}{8}$"

4x4 POST

SECTION DETAIL A

#60

42

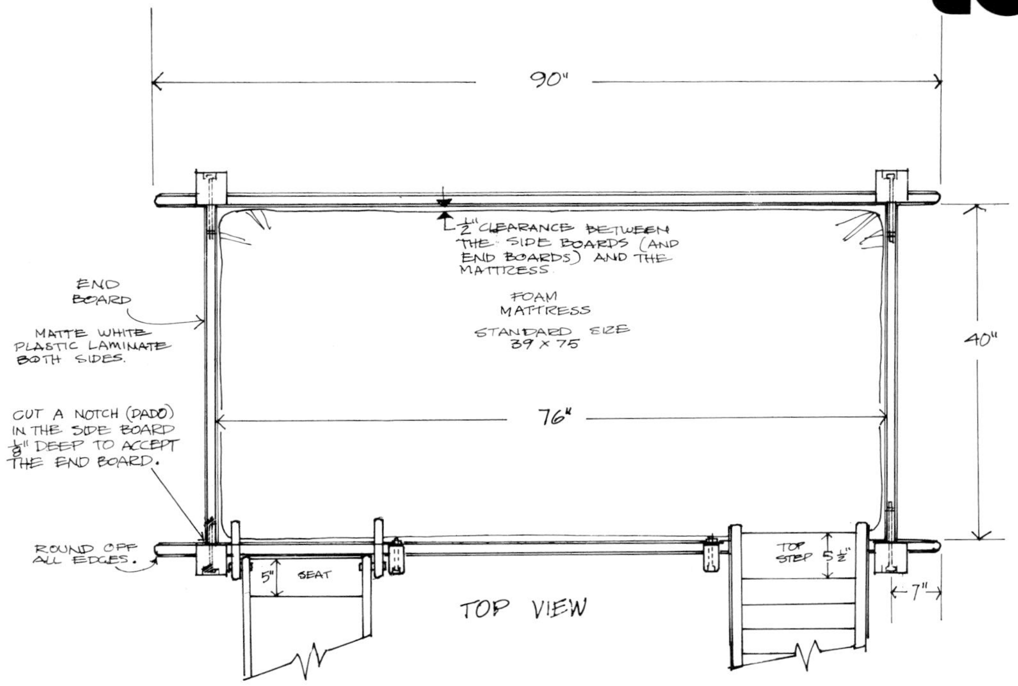

90"

$\frac{1}{2}$" CLEARANCE BETWEEN THE SIDE BOARDS (AND END BOARDS) AND THE MATTRESS.

FOAM MATTRESS
STANDARD SIZE
39 x 75

40"

76"

END BOARD

MATTE WHITE PLASTIC LAMINATE BOTH SIDES.

CUT A NOTCH (DADO) IN THE SIDE BOARD $\frac{3}{8}$" DEEP TO ACCEPT THE END BOARD.

ROUND OFF ALL EDGES.

5" SEAT

TOP STEP 5$\frac{1}{2}$"

7"

TOP VIEW

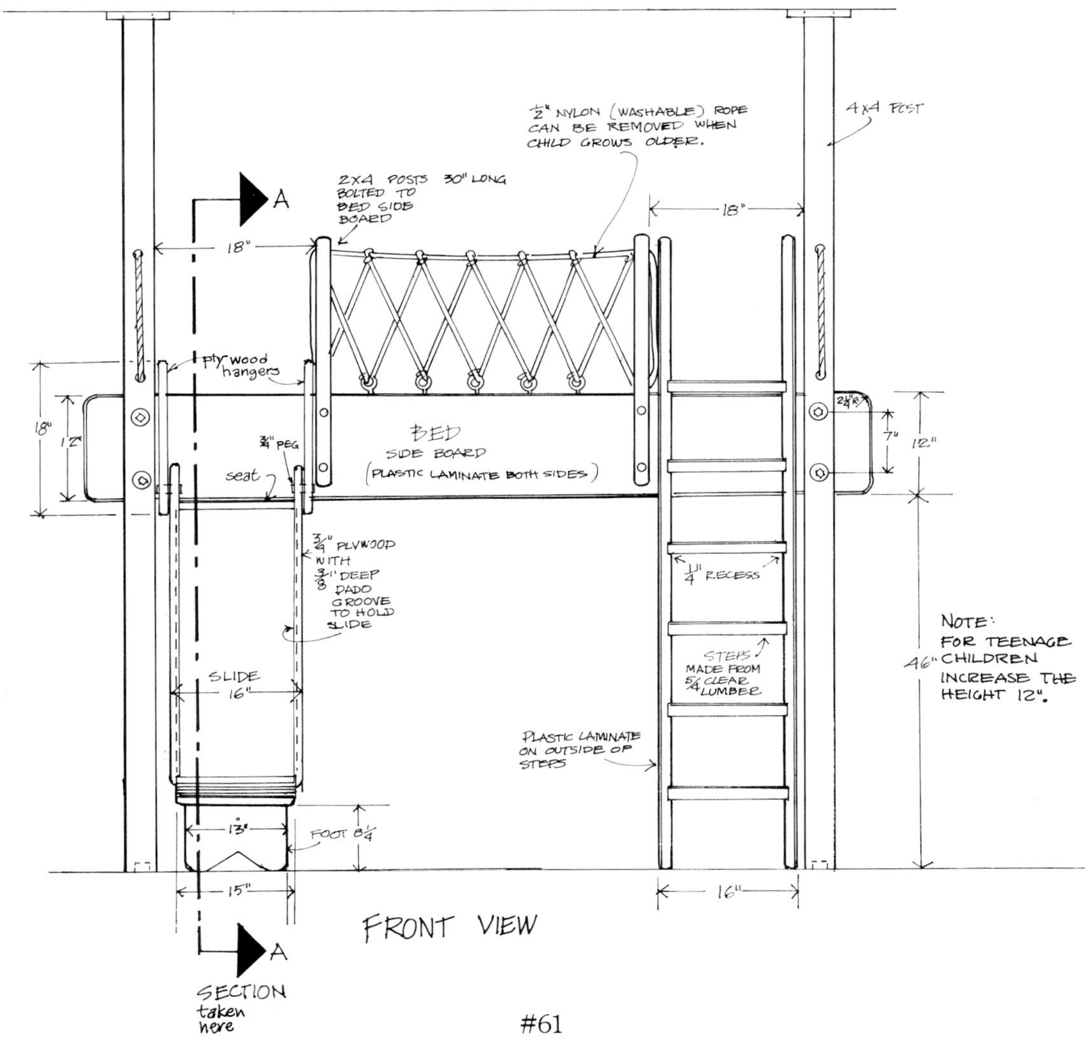

$\frac{1}{2}$" NYLON (WASHABLE) ROPE CAN BE REMOVED WHEN CHILD GROWS OLDER.

4 x 4 POST

2 x 4 POSTS 30" LONG BOLTED TO BED SIDE BOARD

18"

18"

plywood hangers

18"

12"

BED SIDE BOARD
(PLASTIC LAMINATE BOTH SIDES)

$\frac{3}{4}$" PEG

seat

$\frac{3}{4}$" PLYWOOD WITH $\frac{3}{8}$" DEEP DADO GROOVE TO HOLD SLIDE

SLIDE 16"

2$\frac{1}{4}$"

7" 12"

$\frac{1}{4}$" RECESS

STEPS MADE FROM 5/4 CLEAR LUMBER

PLASTIC LAMINATE ON OUTSIDE OF STEPS

NOTE:
FOR TEENAGE CHILDREN INCREASE THE HEIGHT 12".

46"

13"

FOOT 6$\frac{1}{4}$"

15"

16"

FRONT VIEW

A

A

SECTION taken here

#61

LOFT BED

together. Check to see whether the posts are squarely aligned by measuring the diagonals (they should be the same). Tighten up the bolts and screw the ceiling brackets into the ceiling.

Screw four pieces of 1 x 1 in. aluminum angle extrusion to form a lip on the inside of the bed. Cut the 3/4 in. plywood bed bottom to the right size, lay it inside the bed, and screw it to the aluminum angle extrusion (see detail A, illus. #60).

Buy a standard 39 x 75 in. foam mattress, lay it on the bed bottom, and cover it with a contour bed sheet.

Finishing the Posts

For a really nice job you might want to sand and finish the posts with polyurethane so they won't get fingerprints and scuff marks on them. However, this task may take the longest of all the steps to do — even with a belt sander — because each side must be sanded *three times* using coarse, medium, and fine grades of sandpaper. Each post has four sides, times four posts, equals sixteen sides 8 ft. long or 128 ft. times three sandings equals 384 ft. of sanding to do. A lot of work! You can upgrade the wood you are using by drilling out any ugly knots with a 1 in. flat spade drill and filling with wood putty. This gives the post a more consistent, clear look.

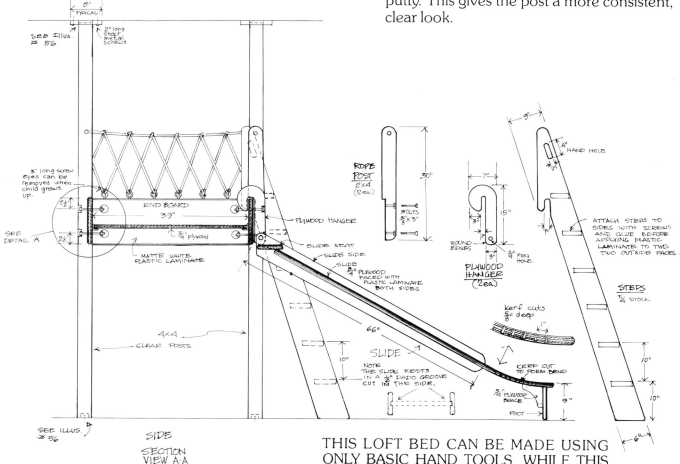

THIS LOFT BED CAN BE MADE USING ONLY BASIC HAND TOOLS, WHILE THIS SLIDE AND STEPS REQUIRE AN ELECTRIC ROUTER TO MAKE THE DADO GROOVES. TO AVOID BUYING AN EXPENSIVE ROUTER, YOU CAN ELIMINATE THE SLIDE AND MAKE THE STEPS WITH BUTT JOINTS RATHER THAN RECESSED JOINTS AS SHOWN.

LOFT BED

INFANT CARRIER

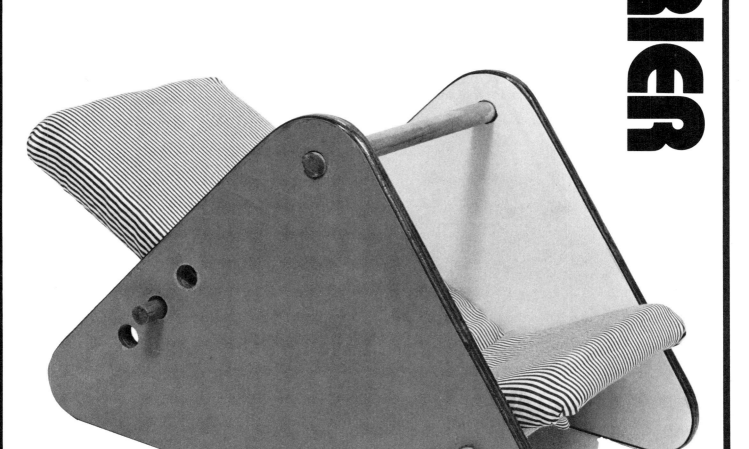

SEATING

INFANT CARRIER

The infant carrier is made to hold a young baby (up to 6 months old) for feeding, sleeping, or carrying from place to place. By changing the back dowel, the seat can be adjusted for three positions: sleeping, eating, or upright. It is made of lightweight 1/2 in. and 3/8 in. thick plywood and weighs only six pounds. It takes about a day to make and requires no screws or nails to hold it together. The seat can be easily taken apart for carrying or for flat storage. Unlike other baby carriers on the market, this one cannot tip over, due to the low center of gravity and the wide base. The handle can be used to attach objects for the baby to play with, and he or she can use it to do pull-ups, thus strengthening the arms and stomach muscles.

How to Make the Infant Carrier

Start with the back and the seat. Following the contours shown in the plan (illus. #63 and #64), saw the pieces out of 3/8 in. plywood using a saber saw. You'll find that the back piece fits into the slot in the rear of the seat. This is a loose fit and should allow the back to hinge back and forth. To obtain a greater degree of inclination, it's necessary to cut away at an angle the edges that touch, so that the seat and the back form a 135° angle when laid down as flat as they will go (see illus. #65).

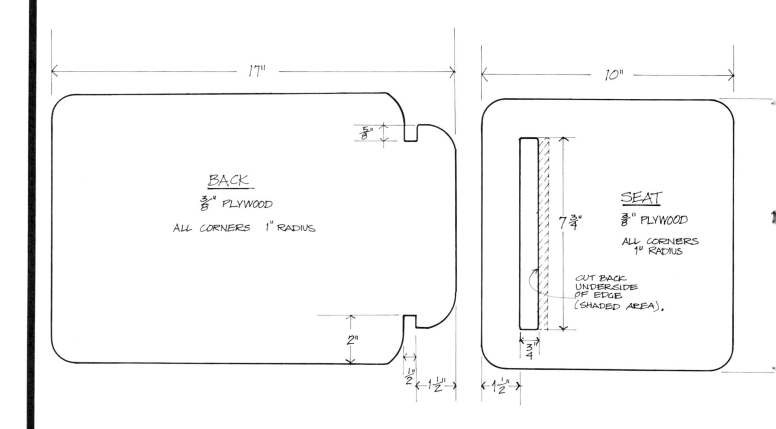

#63

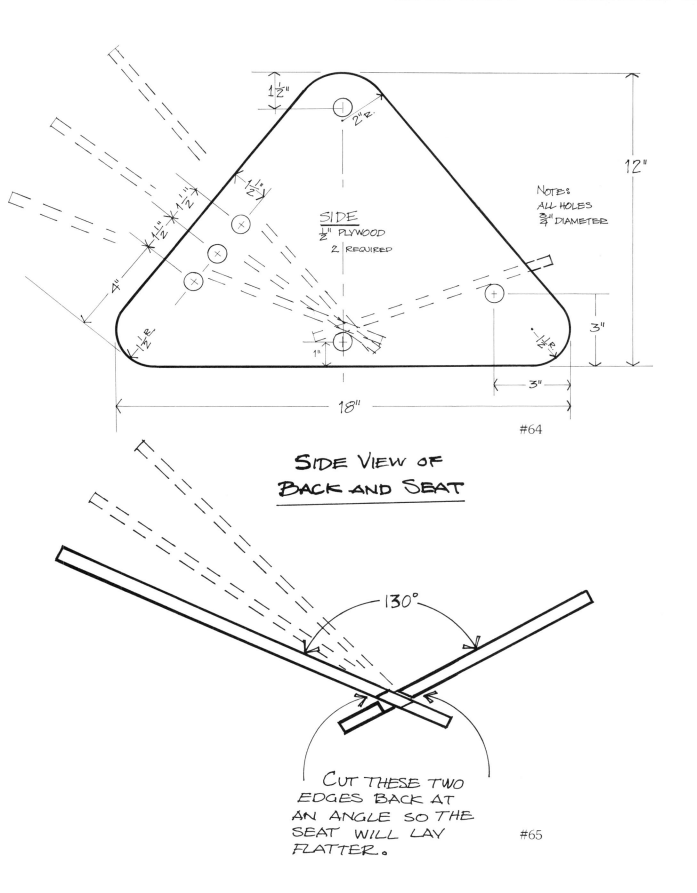

1 1/2"

2" R.

12"

1 1/2"

1 1/2"

NOTE:
ALL HOLES
3/4" DIAMETER

SIDE
1/2" PLYWOOD
2 REQUIRED

1 1/2"

4"

1/2" R.

3"

1"

1/2" R.

3"

18"

#64

SIDE VIEW OF
BACK AND SEAT

130°

CUT THESE TWO
EDGES BACK AT
AN ANGLE SO THE
SEAT WILL LAY
FLATTER.

#65

INFANT CARRIER

The sides are cut from 1/2 in. plywood. Be sure to fill any voids that may appear in the edge of the plywood with wood putty and sand the edges smooth. If you are using plastic laminate, apply it to both sides of each side piece and then round off the edges. Then drill the 3/4 in. holes as shown in the plan (illus. #64). The dowels should fit tightly except the rear one, which should be 5/8 in. diameter and should fit loosely so that it can be slipped in and out easily. To keep it in place, drill a 1/4 in. hole in each end and insert a 1/4 in. diameter removable peg. Place the seat on the frame so that the part where the seat crosses the back rests directly on the bottom cross dowel.

Note: When drilling the holes for the dowels, use a back-up piece of scrap wood clamped under the piece you are drilling to minimize splintering around the hole.

For the seat, a soft pad is cut from a piece of 1 in. foam rubber (sold in most fabric or furniture stores) and is covered with any washable material, such as nylon. Cut the material 4 in. oversize on each side and make a 1/2 in. hem around it to hold a drawstring. When placing the back and seat on the frame, make sure there is clearance for the material by adjusting the dowels. The material wraps around to the back and is tied with a drawstring (illus. #67).

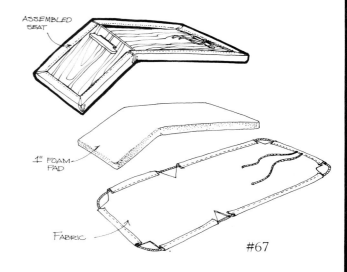

SEAT FOR CARRIER

UPSIDE-DOWN VIEW

ASSEMBLED SEAT

1" FOAM PAD

FABRIC

#67

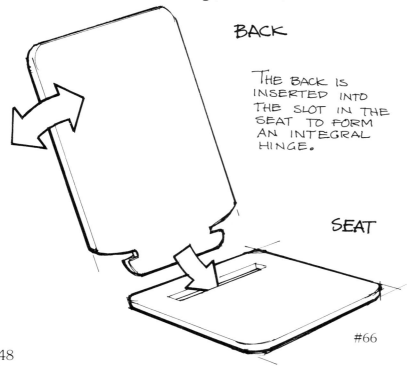

BACK

THE BACK IS INSERTED INTO THE SLOT IN THE SEAT TO FORM AN INTEGRAL HINGE.

SEAT

#66

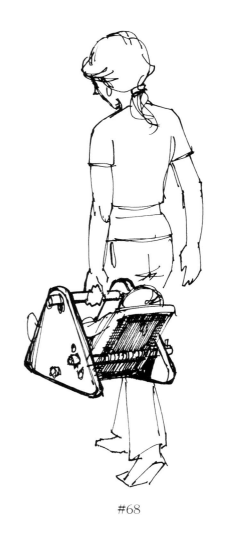

#68

HIGH CHAIR

HIGH CHAIR

For those willing to break away from the traditional high chair, this versatile chair may be the answer. With no legs for tipping or getting in the way of the mop, your baby's spills can be quickly sponged away. This lightweight but sturdy high chair can be lifted easily from its wall bracket and placed outside, on the porch, on the kitchen counter, or anywhere you like. In order to mount the bracket, some holes must be made in the wall, but the convenience of this legless design compensates for patching these later.

How to Make the High Chair

Very little material is needed to make this high chair. It can all be cut from a 15 x 48 in. piece of 1/2 in. plywood (see cutting plan, illus. #69). In addition, you will need white glue, a box of 1-1/2 in. finishing nails, and sandpaper. The surface of the tray should be covered with a piece of white plastic laminate 13 x 8 in. The wall bracket requires one piece of 3/4 in. thick wood 3 x 11 in., one 3/8 in. diameter 3-1/2 in. long flat-head screw, and four 2 in. long sheet metal screws. The material for the whole project should be a little over $10 (1979 prices).

Cut out all the pieces shown on the cutting plan. Use a coping saw for the round corners, or use an electric saber saw if you have one. Fill all the voids in the edge of the plywood with wood filler and sand the edges smooth. Cover all the exposed surfaces with spackle paste except for the edges and top of tray, which will be covered later with plastic laminate. This will hide the imperfections on the surface of the plywood. Use a 4 in. wide spackling knife and spread it as smoothly as possible. When the spackle dries, sand the surface, using a piece of medium sandpaper wrapped around a flat block of wood. Repeat this step with a second application.

Cut a 1/2 in. wide, 1/4 in. deep dado groove 7-1/2 in. from the bottom of the sides (see plan side view, illus. #71). This is easily done if you have an electric router but takes a little longer if you do it by hand. To

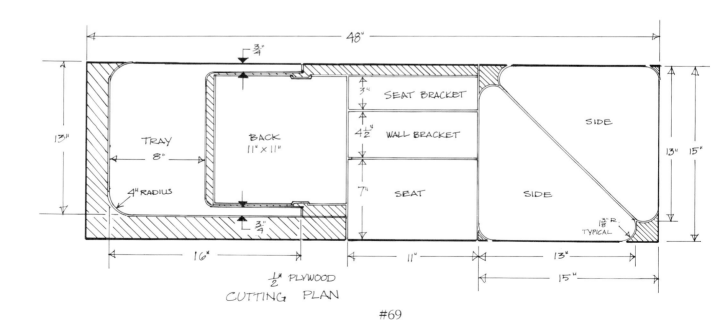

CUTTING PLAN

#69

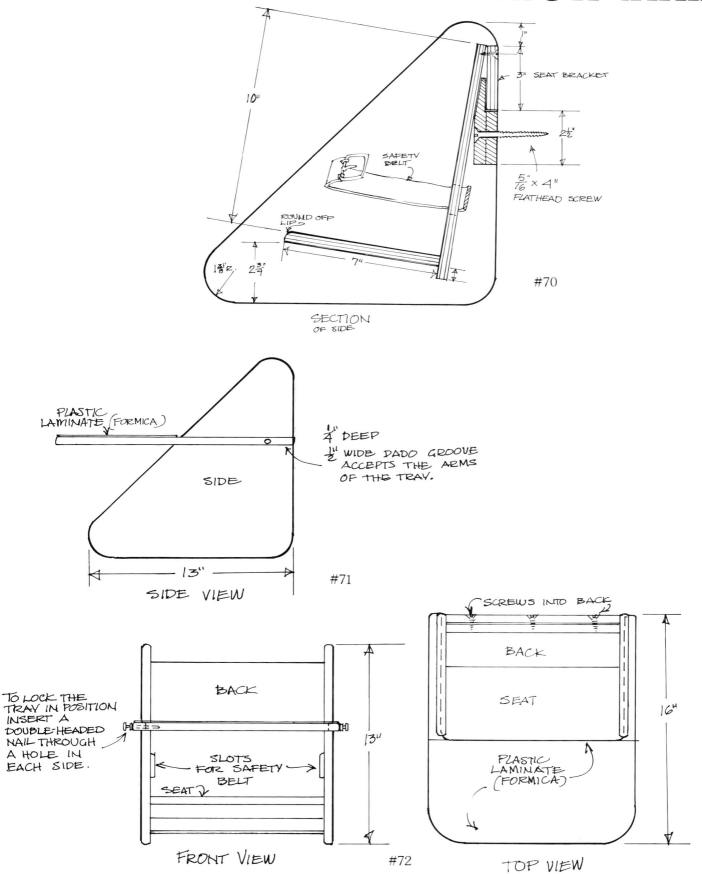

10"

3" SEAT BRACKET

2½"

$\frac{5}{16}$" × 4" FLATHEAD SCREW

SAFETY BELT

ROUND OFF LIPS

1⅜"R.   2¾"   7"

#70

SECTION OF SIDE

PLASTIC LAMINATE (FORMICA)

$\frac{1}{4}$" DEEP
$\frac{1}{2}$" WIDE DADO GROOVE ACCEPTS THE ARMS OF THE TRAY.

SIDE

13"

#71

SIDE VIEW

SCREWS INTO BACK

BACK

SEAT

16"

PLASTIC LAMINATE (FORMICA)

TO LOCK THE TRAY IN POSITION INSERT A DOUBLE-HEADED NAIL THROUGH A HOLE IN EACH SIDE.

BACK

13"

SLOTS FOR SAFETY BELT

SEAT

FRONT VIEW

#72

TOP VIEW

HIGH CHAIR

make it by hand, mark the two lines on the side and carefully start two straight cuts with a hand dado saw (see illus. #73).

Cut the dado joint out with a chisel so that it's 1/4 in. deep. Smooth the inside with sandpaper so that the tray slides in and out smoothly. Assemble all the pieces with glue and 1-1/2 in. finishing nails. Don't drive the nails all the way in until you've checked to see that everything fits properly. Then drive the nails all the way in and recess them with a nail set. Fill the nail holes and any remaining cracks with spackle. When the spackle has dried thoroughly, sand everything smooth.

Next, paint the chair with a high-grade spray enamel. Be sure to spray *away* from the edges. To avoid drips spray only the horizontal surfaces. When they have dried, turn the piece and spray the next horizontal sur-

faces. Repeat until all surfaces have at least three coats. Take your time during the painting process and allow an hour between each spraying.

Round the edges and sand until absolutely smooth. Give them three coats of polyurethane.

The wall bracket is attached by finding the 2 x 4 stud behind the wall and screwing a 3/8 x 3-1/2 in. flathead screw through the plaster into the wood stud. As an added precaution, insert four sheet metal screws into the corners of the bracket (see illus. #75). If your wall is masonry, use lead masonry anchors.

When your child outgrows the high chair and the time comes to remove the bracket from the wall, simply unscrew it and patch the holes as explained on page 66.

CUTTING THE DADO GROOVE

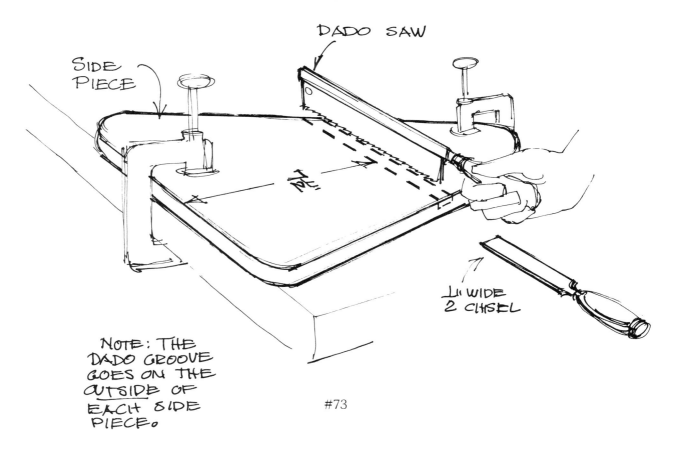

SIDE PIECE

DADO SAW

NOTE: THE DADO GROOVE GOES ON THE OUTSIDE OF EACH SIDE PIECE.

1" WIDE 2 CHISEL

#73

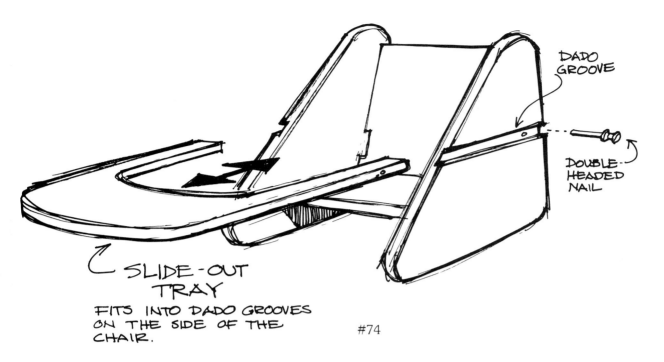

DADO
GROOVE

DOUBLE-
HEADED
NAIL

SLIDE-OUT
TRAY

FITS INTO DADO GROOVES
ON THE SIDE OF THE
CHAIR.

#74

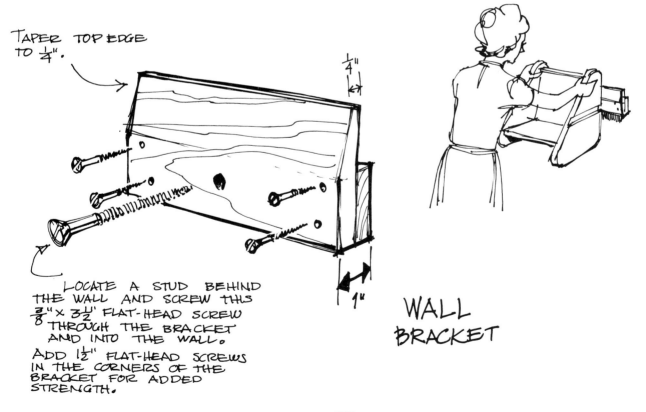

TAPER TOP EDGE
TO $\frac{1}{4}$".

$\frac{1}{4}$"

1"

WALL
BRACKET

LOCATE A STUD BEHIND
THE WALL AND SCREW THIS
$\frac{3}{8}$" X $3\frac{1}{2}$" FLAT-HEAD SCREW
THROUGH THE BRACKET
AND INTO THE WALL.

ADD $1\frac{1}{2}$" FLAT-HEAD SCREWS
IN THE CORNERS OF THE
BRACKET FOR ADDED
STRENGTH.

#75

STORAGE CHAIR

STORAGE CHAIR

The storage chair is both a chair and a toy. Children will like pushing it around the house, and it can be a shopping cart for kids helping Mom or Dad with the groceries. For 1-year-olds it is a good way to learn how to walk. After an infant learns to stand, he can steady himself by holding onto the top rail and walking around the house. Make sure the infant starts learning on a carpet or heavy pile rug as the chair might roll too quickly on a hard floor.

How to Make the Storage Chair

1. From a piece of 3/4 in. plywood cut the backrest, back, front, and sides according to the cutting plan below. Refer to Section View of Side shown in illus. #78 and round off the corners with a saber saw. Drill 1 in. holes in each side as shown in the section (illus. #78).

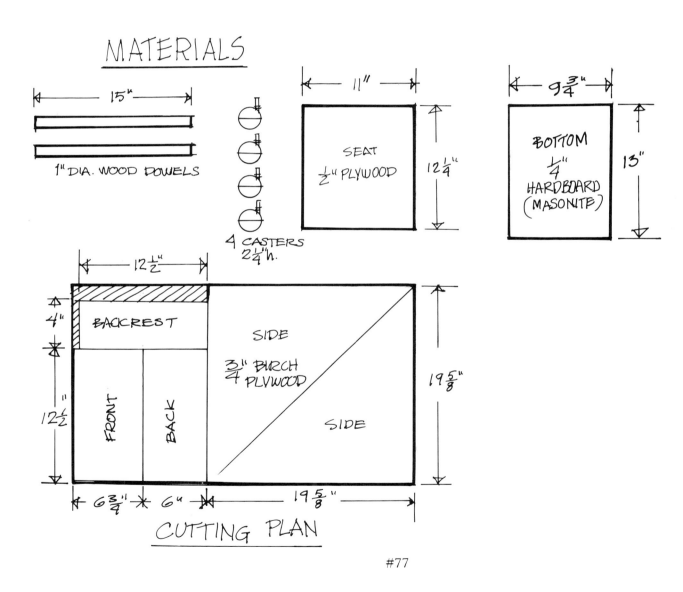

MATERIALS

15"

1" DIA. WOOD DOWELS

4 CASTERS 2¼" h.

11"

SEAT ½" PLYWOOD

12¼"

9¾"

BOTTOM ¼" HARDBOARD (MASONITE)

13"

12½"

4"

BACKREST

12½"

FRONT

BACK

SIDE

¾" BIRCH PLYWOOD

SIDE

19⅝"

6¾"   6"   19⅝"

CUTTING PLAN

#77

56

STORAGE CHAIR

- FITS UNDER WORK TABLE.
- STORAGE FOR SUPPLIES UNDER SEAT.
- USED AS A PUSH-TOY (WALKER) BY THE CHILD TO IMITATE MOMMY'S SHOPPING CART.

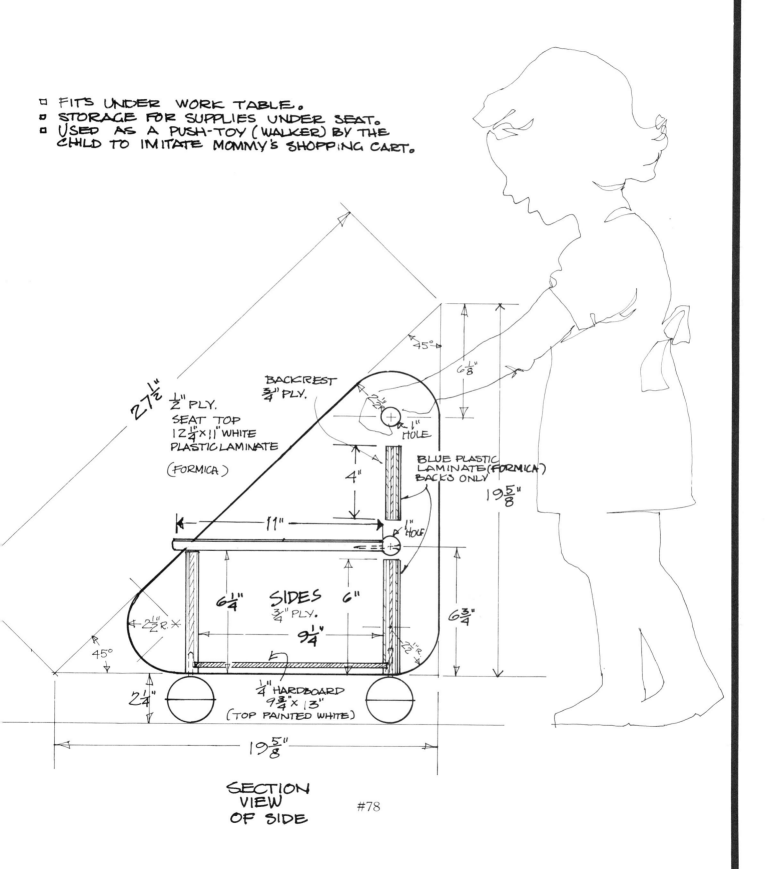

$27\frac{1}{2}$"

$\frac{1}{2}$" PLY.
SEAT TOP
$12\frac{1}{4}$"×11" WHITE
PLASTIC LAMINATE

(FORMICA)

BACKREST
$\frac{3}{4}$" PLY.

45°

$6\frac{1}{8}$"

$2\frac{1}{2}$"R.

1" HOLE

4"

11"

BLUE PLASTIC
LAMINATE (FORMICA)
BACKS ONLY

1" HOLE

$19\frac{5}{8}$"

SIDES
$\frac{3}{4}$" PLY.

$6\frac{1}{4}$"

6"

$9\frac{1}{4}$"

$6\frac{3}{4}$"

$2\frac{1}{2}$"R.

45°

$2\frac{1}{2}$"R.

$2\frac{1}{4}$"

$\frac{1}{4}$" HARDBOARD
$9\frac{3}{4}$"× 13"
(TOP PAINTED WHITE)

$19\frac{5}{8}$"

SECTION
VIEW
OF SIDE

#78

STORAGE CHAIR

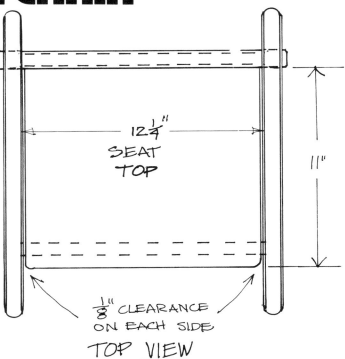

12 1/4"
SEAT
TOP

11"

1/8" CLEARANCE
ON EACH SIDE

TOP VIEW

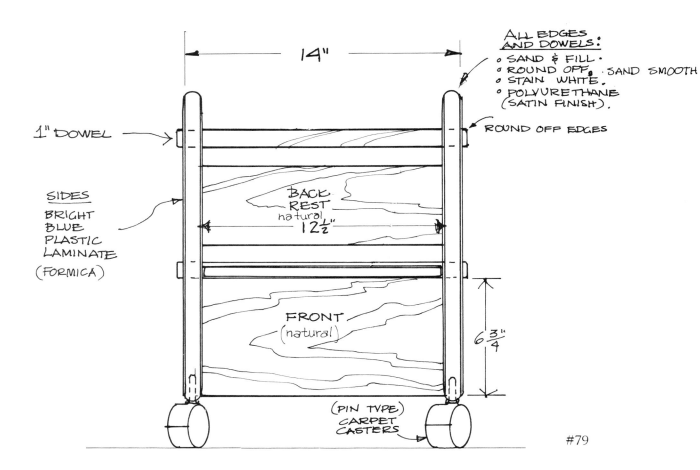

14"

ALL EDGES
AND DOWELS:
o SAND & FILL.
o ROUND OFF. · SAND SMOOTH
o STAIN WHITE.
o POLYURETHANE
(SATIN FINISH).

ROUND OFF EDGES

1" DOWEL

SIDES
BRIGHT
BLUE
PLASTIC
LAMINATE
(FORMICA)

BACK
REST
natural
12 1/2"

FRONT
(natural)

6 3/4"

(PIN TYPE)
CARPET
CASTERS

#79

FRONT

2. Cut the seat from 1/2 in. plywood and glue a piece of plastic laminate to the top. Round off the edges (see illus. #80).

3. Cut two pieces of 1 in. diameter wooden dowel 15 in. long and flatten one side (see illus. #81), leaving 1-3/8 in. round on each end. Nail and glue the dowel to the back edge of the seat.

4. With a router or dado saw cut a 1/4 in. wide, 1/4 in. deep groove 1/2 in. from the bottom of each side, front, and back to accept the hardboard (Masonite) bottom. If you don't have a router or dado saw, you can substitute 1/2 in. plywood for the bottom; in this case the bottom should be 9-1/4 x 12-1/2 in.

5. Before you assemble the pieces, lay the two sides down on two pieces of plastic laminate and mark where the holes should be. Cut the holes in the plastic laminate with a 1 in. hole saw.

6. Glue and nail everything together, being careful not to get glue on the wooden hinge dowel. When this is dry, glue plastic laminate to both sides.

7. Round off the edges, sand smooth, and finish with three coats of polyurethane.

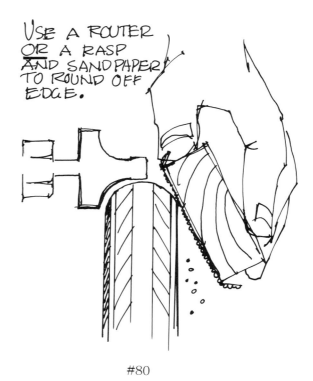

USE A ROUTER OR A RASP AND SANDPAPER TO ROUND OFF EDGE.

#80

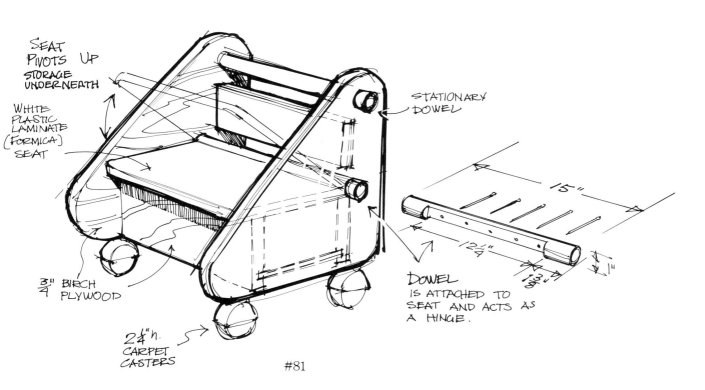

SEAT PIVOTS UP
STORAGE UNDERNEATH

WHITE PLASTIC LAMINATE (FORMICA) SEAT

STATIONARY DOWEL

3/4" BIRCH PLYWOOD

2 4/4" n. CARPET CASTERS

DOWEL IS ATTACHED TO SEAT AND ACTS AS A HINGE.

15"

12 1/4"

1 3/8"

1"

#81

CHANGING TABLE

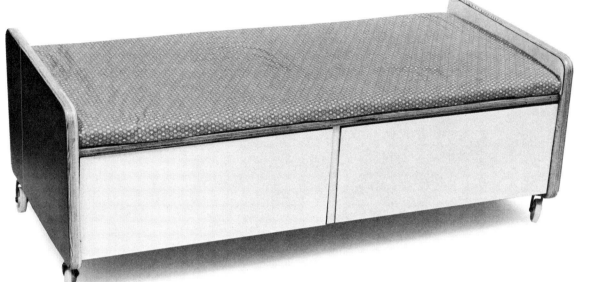

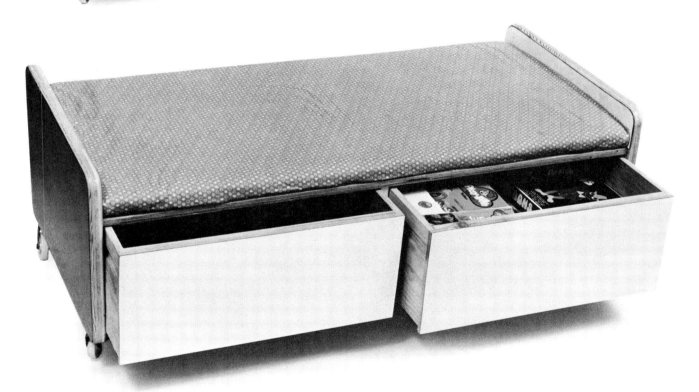

TABLES

CHANGING TABLE

The changing table is a necessary piece of equipment in any baby's room. Its function is to provide a convenient and safe place to rest the baby while changing diapers. The two advantages of this design over store-bought versions are that it is wall mounted, making it easier to clean underneath, and that it can be converted in a matter of minutes into a convenient storage bench by taking it off the wall and adding casters (see illus. #83).

The changing table is easier to make if you have an electric router; however, just to prove it could be done without electric tools, I asked my wife to cut the dado grooves with a dado hand saw and chisel, which she succeeded in doing without much difficulty. Be prepared to spend two to three hours of hard work if you decide to try it this way.

Note: The dado grooves are only necessary if you plan to hang the changing table on the wall. Otherwise you can use simple butt joints.

How to Make the Changing Table

From a sheet of 1/2 in. plywood, cut

Two sides	12 x 18 in.
Top	17-1/2 x 36 in.
Back	7-3/4 x 36-1/2 in.
Bottom	16-1/4 x 36 in.
Center divider	7-1/4 x 16 in. (notch out the back top)

Note: Be very careful when cutting the center divider; it must be absolutely square and accurate to within 1/16 in.

Cut 1/2 in. dado grooves in the inside faces of the top and bottom pieces, 1/2 in. from the back edge.

Cut a 1/2 in. wide x 1/4 in. deep dado groove on the inside faces of the side pieces, 3/4 in. from the back edge. Stop the dado cut 3/4 in. from the top.

CHANGING TABLE

- HANGS ON THE WALL SO BABY HAS MORE FLOOR SPACE TO CRAWL.
- HAS TWO DRAWERS FOR DIAPERS, BLANKETS, CLOTHES, ETC.
- CONVERTS INTO STORAGE BIN FOR TOYS AFTER THE BABY OUTGROWS IT.

#82

CHANGING TABLE CONVERTED TO TOY STORAGE SEAT

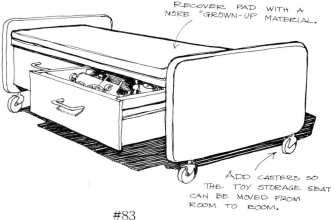

RECOVER PAD WITH A MORE "GROWN-UP" MATERIAL.

ADD CASTERS SO THE TOY STORAGE SEAT CAN BE MOVED FROM ROOM TO ROOM.

#83

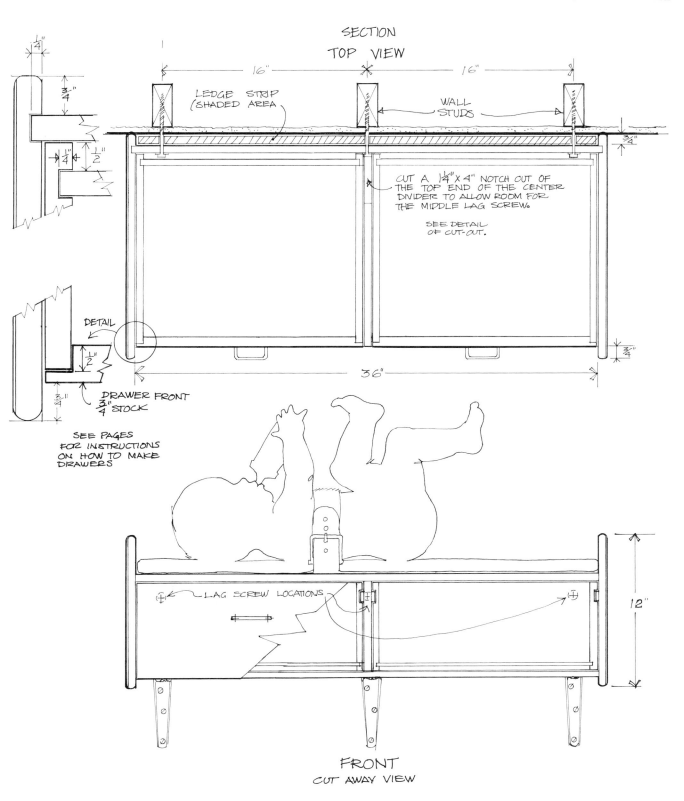

SECTION
TOP VIEW

16"   16"

LEDGE STRIP
(SHADED AREA

WALL
STUDS

CUT A 1¼"X 4" NOTCH OUT OF
THE TOP END OF THE CENTER
DIVIDER TO ALLOW ROOM FOR
THE MIDDLE LAG SCREW.

SEE DETAIL
OF CUT-OUT.

¼"

¾"

¼"   ½"

¾"

36"

¾"

DETAIL

½"

¾"

DRAWER FRONT
¾"STOCK

SEE PAGES
FOR INSTRUCTIONS
ON HOW TO MAKE
DRAWERS

LAG SCREW LOCATIONS

12"

FRONT
CUT AWAY VIEW

#84

CHANGING TABLE

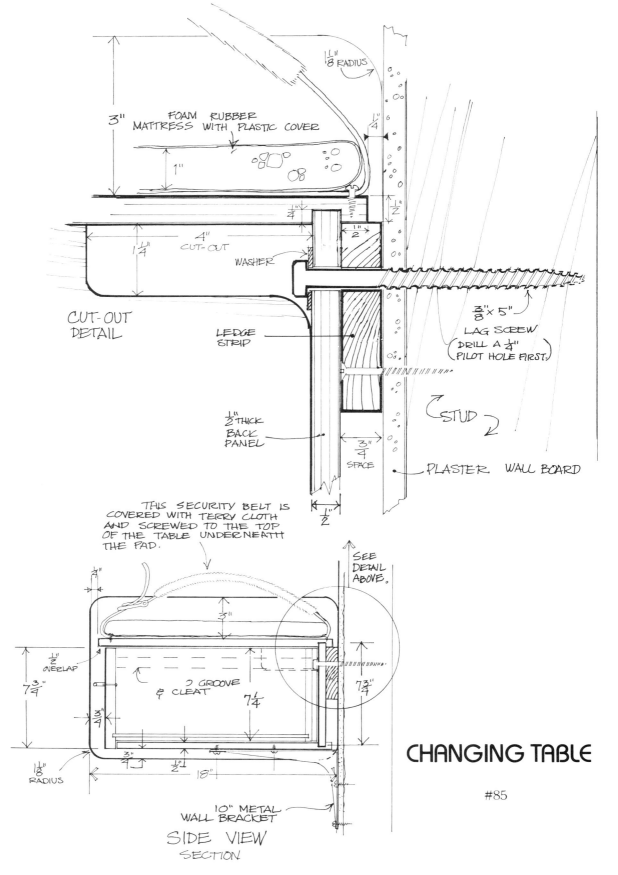

$\frac{1}{8}$" RADIUS

3" FOAM RUBBER MATTRESS WITH PLASTIC COVER

1"

$\frac{1}{4}$"

$\frac{1}{2}$"

$\frac{1}{4}$"

CUT-OUT DETAIL

$1\frac{1}{4}$"

4" CUT-OUT

$\frac{1}{4}$"

1" 2

WASHER

LEDGE STRIP

$\frac{1}{2}$" THICK BACK PANEL

$\frac{3}{4}$" SPACE

$\frac{3}{8}$"× 5" LAG SCREW (DRILL A $\frac{1}{4}$" PILOT HOLE FIRST.)

STUD

PLASTER WALL BOARD

$\frac{1}{2}$"

THIS SECURITY BELT IS COVERED WITH TERRY CLOTH AND SCREWED TO THE TOP OF THE TABLE UNDERNEATH THE PAD.

SEE DETAIL ABOVE.

3"

$\frac{1}{4}$"

$\frac{1}{2}$" OVERLAP

$7\frac{3}{4}$"

2 GROOVE & CLEAT

$7\frac{1}{4}$"

$7\frac{3}{4}$"

$\frac{3}{4}$"

$\frac{3}{4}$"

$\frac{1}{2}$"

18"

$1\frac{1}{8}$" RADIUS

10" METAL WALL BRACKET

SIDE VIEW SECTION

CHANGING TABLE

#85

Assemble all the pieces together without glue to see if they all are accurate and fit perfectly. Lay the bottom down and mark the center line 18 in. from both ends. Draw two lines 1/4 in. on either side of the center line to indicate where the center divider should go. Do the same for the top piece. Glue and nail the center divider to the top and bottom piece after setting the back in the dado grooves along the top and bottom pieces. Attach the two side pieces so that the back fits into the dado grooves, then glue and nail. Apply plastic laminate to the two sides and round off the edges. Sand everything smooth and finish with polyurethane. See pages 13–17 for details on making the drawers. If you wish, you can disregard the drawers and leave the shelf open.

Before you start this project, decide where on the wall you want to hang the changing table. Since it is secured to the wall by three large screws, it is important to know exactly where the studs are behind the wall. Just drilling into plaster won't do. There are many gadgets on the market designed to help you find the studs hidden behind the wall, but the simplest method is this:

1. Since most (but not all) houses built after World War II have studs spaced at 16 in. intervals on center, measure from the nearest corner 16 in. increments and mark where you think the stud should be.

2. Pound the wall with your fist and listen for the solidest sound.

3. To prevent the possibility of accidental shock, turn off the electricity in that section of the house at the fuse box or circuit breaker.

4. Drive a long nail into the wall where you think the stud should be. If it hits something solid and is difficult to remove, you've probably found the stud. If not, open up the hole a little and probe with a screwdriver or coat hanger to the left and the right to see if you can feel the stud.

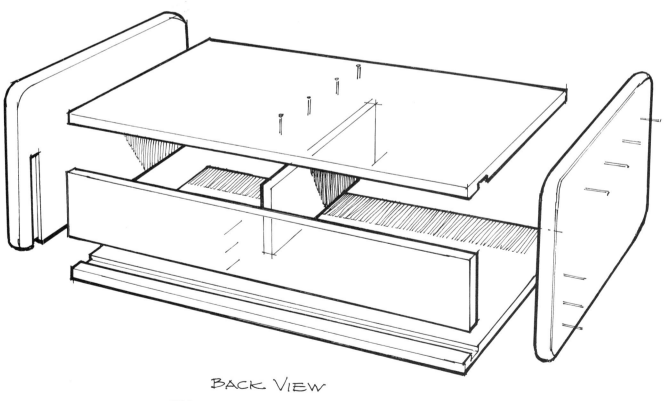

BACK VIEW

#86

5. Mark where you think the stud is and make another exploratory hole. When you're sure you are dead center over the stud, measure over 16 in. (sometimes 20 in. in older houses) and hammer another nail in. If you don't find a stud there, begin the same process over at the new location. If you are apprehensive about punching holes in your nice smooth wall, here are a few tips on patching the holes when you are finished.

Plastering Holes in Walls

Buy a small inexpensive box of plaster spackle and keep it on hand for occasional repair jobs. Spackle is sold wet or dry, and both are good for all kinds of jobs.

Mix the dry spackle to a putty- or dough-like consistency.

Use a 4 in. wide flexible putty knife or a kitchen sandwich spreader or spatula.

Fill the hole with spackle, and after it has set for a few minutes wipe it lightly with a flat wet sponge (see illus. #87). This is all you need to do unless you are a perfectionist, in which case, after the spot has thoroughly dried, sand it with fine sandpaper wrapped around a block of wood. Repeat the process if there are any remaining depressions.

#87

PLASTERING HOLES
LEFT IN WALLS.

ADJUST-TABLE

ADJUST-TABLE

This table is, as the name implies, adjustable. By simply unscrewing four wing nuts (no tools necessary) and repositioning them in a different set of holes, the table height can be raised or lowered to accommodate kids from ages 2 to 6. All the surfaces that are likely to receive severe punishment are covered with plastic laminate. It rests on free-wheeling casters for maximum portability from the dining room to the playroom.

One of my earliest memories is of when I was 3 years old — walking around the house, looking up at the underside of the furniture. Until a child's eyes reach table-top level, it's a pretty drab world. Everything is made for adult dimensions. A visit to a soda fountain reveals the long dark underside of the counter, pockmarked with old chewing gum. The floor, which is much closer to the child's level, is littered with cigarette butts and other debris, and chair legs are filled with cobwebs and spiders. Nothing was my size. Imagine my surprise when my eyes reached the top of our dining-room table and I found it polished! How nice it would have been if somebody had given me a table to eat at that was my size!

This table not only functions as a children's dining table but can also be used as a work table to make cookies, build clay monsters, or draw pictures. It is a good work area for practically any sort of sit-down activity or skill. Even when the child outgrows it, it is attractive enough to be used as a serving table in the dining room.

The Adjust-Table is fairly simple to make and should take no longer than one weekend. It's comprised of two basic parts — the pedestal and the table top. To build it you will need:

3/4 in. plywood

1 piece	24 x 24	top
2 pieces	15 x 7 in.	brackets
2 pieces	21 x 15 in.	sides
1 piece	24 x 7 in.	center divider

This can all be cut out of a half sheet of plywood 48 x 48 in. (4 x 4 ft.).

Plastic laminate

1 piece	24 x 24 in.
2 pieces	21 x 15 in. (preferably of a different color from the top)

Hardware

1	box 2 in. finishing nails
4	3/8 x 2 in. carriage bolts and washers
4	stem-type casters

How to Make the Adjust-Table

To build the Adjust-Table, begin by cutting out all the pieces and rounding off the corners with an electric jigsaw. Cut two slots in the side brackets and drill the holes (as shown in illus. #89) for the side brackets. Glue and nail them onto the table top, making sure they are at right angles to the top. Set aside to dry.

Find the inside center of each side piece and glue and nail sides to the center divider. Place the top on the pedestal so that it will dry in the correct position (see illus. #90).

○ ALL WOOD IS ¾" BIRCH PLYWOOD.

○ ALL EDGES ROUNDED, SANDED, AND PAINTED WITH POLYURETHANE CLEAR GLOSSY LIQUID PLASTIC.

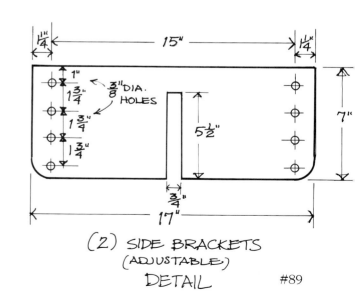

(2) SIDE BRACKETS
(ADJUSTABLE)
DETAIL   #89

ADJUST-TABLE

Cover the table top with plastic laminate, trim off the edges, and sand smooth as described on pages 6–9. Do the same for the two sides. Drill holes for the casters and set them in. Generally they take a 3/8 in. hole, but check to be sure. Give all exposed wood surfaces three coats of polyurethane and make the final assembly with wing nuts.

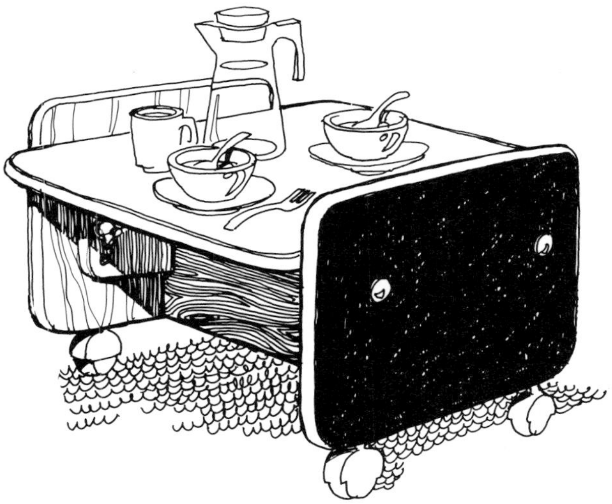

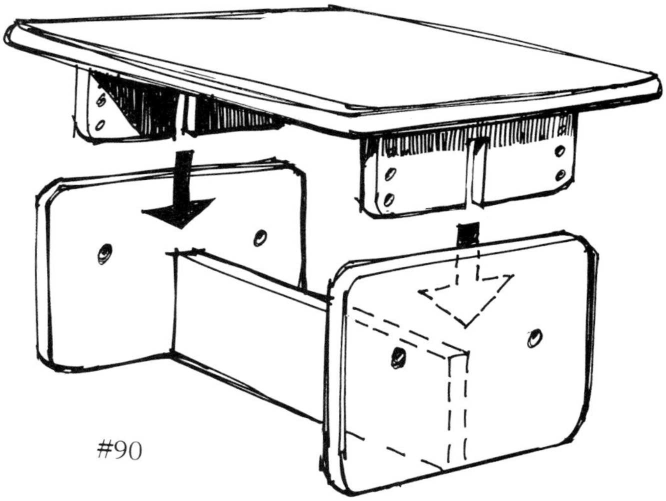

#90

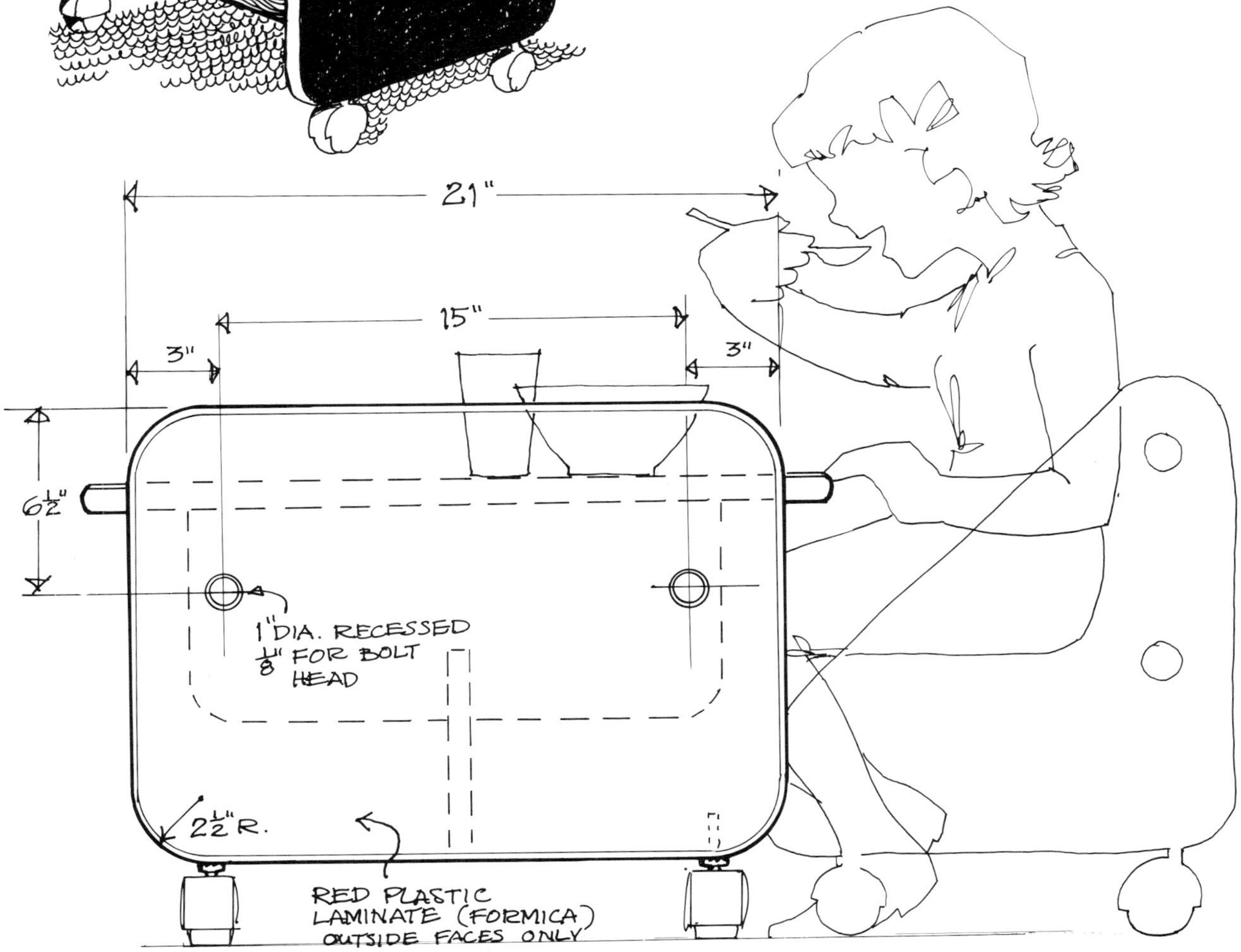

21"
15"
3"
3"
6½"
1" DIA. RECESSED ⅛" FOR BOLT HEAD
2½" R.
RED PLASTIC LAMINATE (FORMICA) OUTSIDE FACES ONLY

SIDE VIEW

#91

ADJUST-TABLE

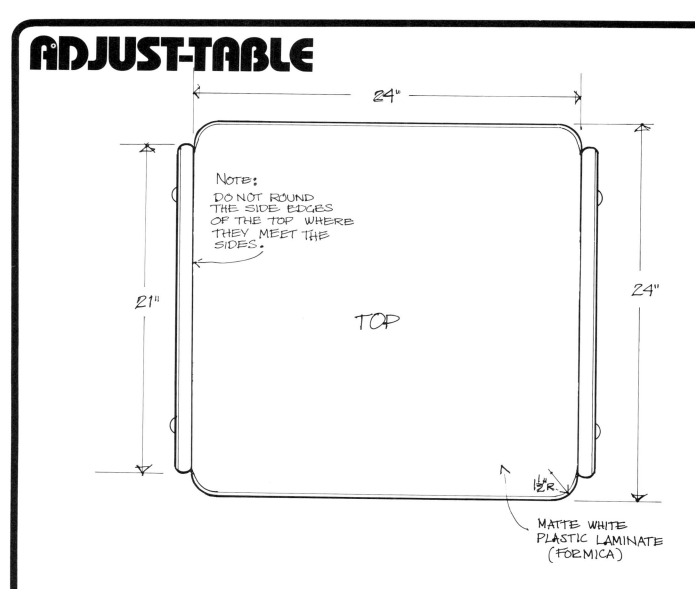

24"

NOTE:

DO NOT ROUND
THE SIDE EDGES
OF THE TOP WHERE
THEY MEET THE
SIDES.

21"

TOP

24"

$1\frac{1}{2}$" R.

MATTE WHITE
PLASTIC LAMINATE
(FORMICA)

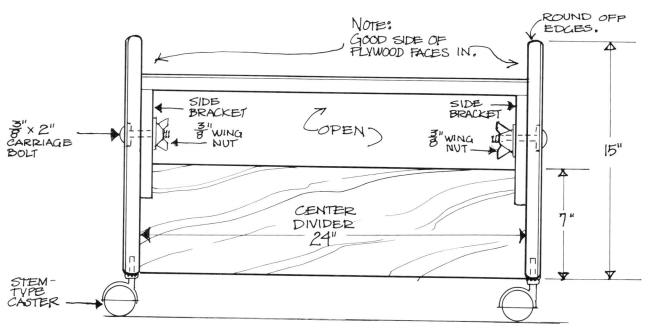

ROUND OFF
EDGES.

NOTE:
GOOD SIDE OF
FLYWOOD FACES IN.

SIDE
BRACKET

$\frac{3}{8}$" WING
NUT

OPEN

SIDE
BRACKET

$\frac{3}{8}$" WING
NUT

$\frac{3}{8}$" × 2"
CARRIAGE
BOLT

15"

CENTER
DIVIDER
24"

7"

STEM-
TYPE
CASTER

FRONT VIEW   #92

TOOL CHEST

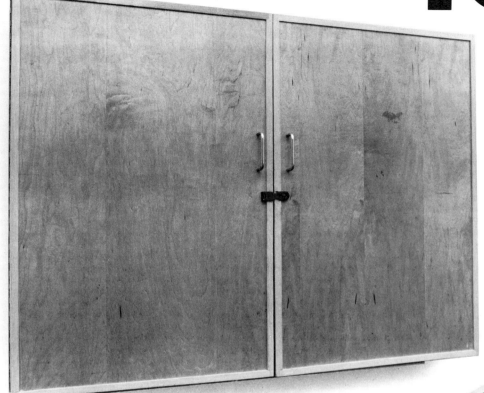

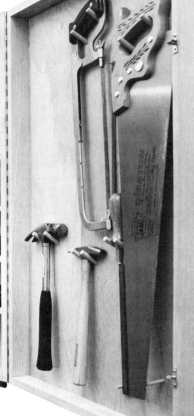

WORK

TOOL CHEST

The tool chest shown here is for any youngster, teenager, or adult who is serious about carpentry and cares about his or her tools. Since 20 percent of a carpenter's time is spent looking for tools, displaying the tools properly is a real time saver. The tool chest can be permanently attached to the wall or closed up and transported to a job. Tools stay sharper longer and are easier to use if kept in a tool chest. It's an excellent gift for a young person who is interested in building. He or she can start with a small collection and gradually acquire more tools as time goes on. New tools fit into the chest easily, since new pegs can be added by boring and gluing them into the 1/2 in. thick backboard.

This project is easy to make, but it does require an electric router or table saw to cut the joints. Clear pine 1 x 4s and 1/2 in. birch plywood are preferred, though cheaper grades of lumber can do a perfectly adequate job. The plastic laminate front is optional.

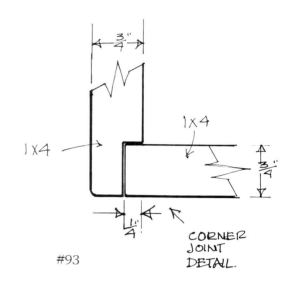

#93

CORNER JOINT DETAIL.

How to Make the Tool Chest

Materials

2 pcs. 1 x 4	8 ft. long (cut 23 in. long pieces)	tops & bottoms
3 pcs. 1 x 4	6 ft. long (cut into 36 in. pieces)	sides
1 pc. 1 x 4	34-1/2 in. long	center divider
4 pcs. 1 x 4	23-3/8 in.	shelves
2 pcs. 1 x 2	22-7/8 in.	rail
1 pc. 1 x 2	48 in. long	wall support
1 pc. 1/2 in. thick plywood 47 x 35 in.		back panel
2 pcs. 1/2 in. thick plywood 23 x 35 in.		side panels
18 glass jars		

Cut all the lumber to size, making sure that the panels are square. Make a 1/2 in. wide, 1/4 in. deep dado groove 1/8 in. from the outside edge of the top and side pieces. Next the sides are rabbeted to accept the top and bottom pieces (see illus. #93).

Mark the shelf positions according to the height of the glass jars you are using to store nails, etc. Cut the dado grooves for the right side piece and the center divider at the same time. Before the final assembly, place all the pieces into their proper positions and check to see that everything fits, making sure that the shelves fit into the grooves.

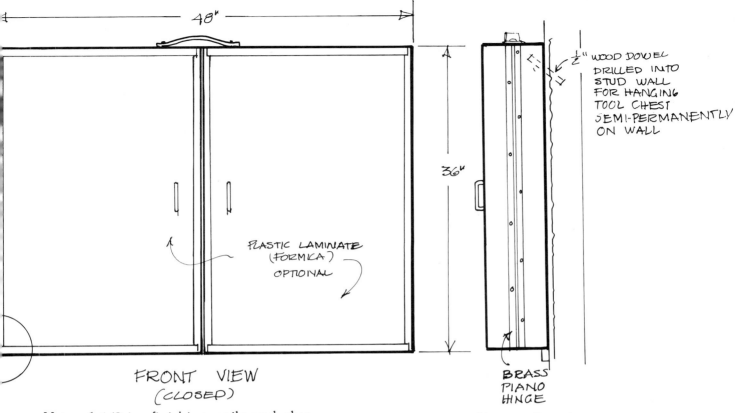

48"

36"

PLASTIC LAMINATE
(FORMICA)
OPTIONAL

FRONT VIEW
(CLOSED)

½" WOOD DOWEL
DRILLED INTO
STUD WALL
FOR HANGING
TOOL CHEST
SEMI-PERMANENTLY
ON WALL

BRASS
PIANO
HINGE

#94   SIDE VIEW

Using 1-1/2 in. finishing nails and glue, assemble the cabinet and doors. Check frequently for squareness. When the glue is dry, screw the center divider into the cabinet and slide the shelves into place. It's better not to glue them, since you may want to remove them later and rearrange your storage space. Glue and nail the 1 x 2 rails in place (see plan for illus. #95). Add friction catches, door handles, and a piece of 1/4 in. thick leather for a carrying handle.

Now comes the fun part. Gather together your tool collection and lay the tool chest down on the floor. Begin placing your tools in the chest, marking with a light pencil where they will be stored. Leave space for tools that you plan to buy in the future. Most of the tools can be hung by boring a 3/8 in. diameter hole partway into the 1/2 in. plywood. Put pegs in at a consistent upward angle by making a jig (see illus. #97).

Wood pegs are chosen to hang the tools on rather than pegboard wire brackets because they are cheaper and make a nice "thud" when the tool is returned to its place rather than a "clank."

TOOL CHEST

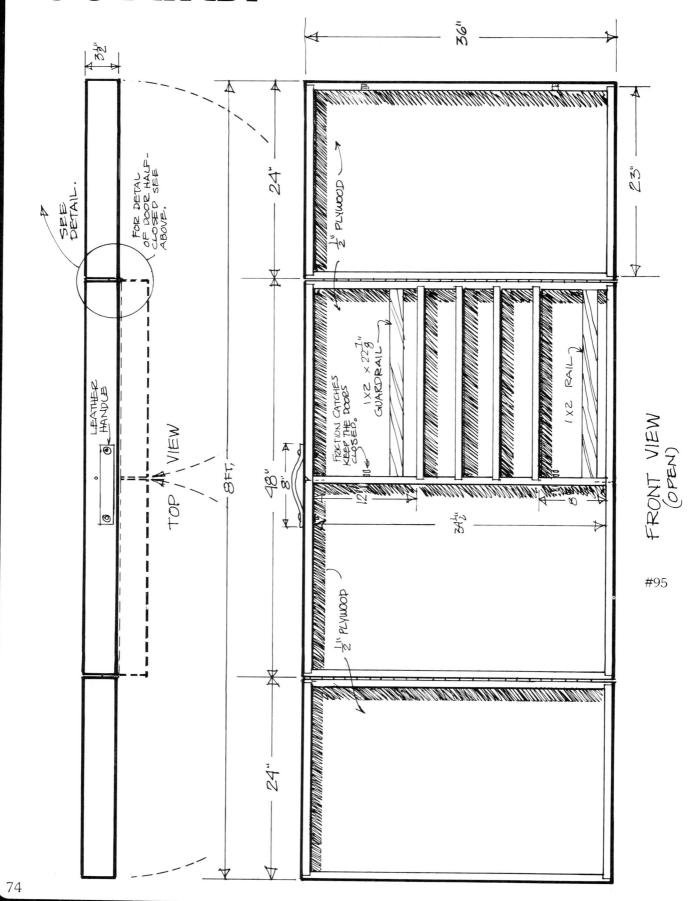

SEE DETAIL.

FOR DETAIL OF DOOR HALF-CLOSED SEE ABOVE.

LEATHER HANDLE

TOP VIEW

$3\frac{1}{2}$"

8 FT.

36"

24"

23"

$\frac{1}{2}$" PLYWOOD

FRICTION CATCHES KEEP THE DOORS CLOSED.

1 X 2 × $22\frac{7}{8}$" GUARDRAIL

1 X 2 RAIL

48"

8"

$34\frac{1}{2}$"

$\frac{1}{2}$" PLYWOOD

24"

FRONT VIEW (OPEN)

#95

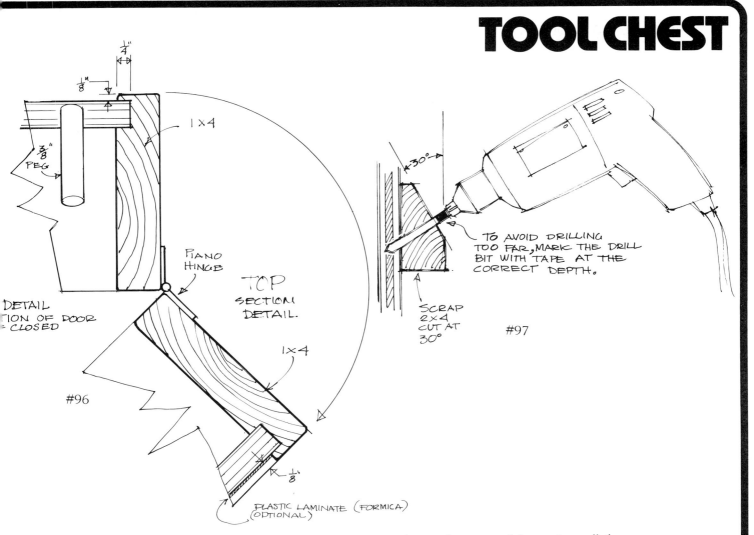

¼"

⅛"

3/8"
PEG

1 X 4

DETAIL
TION OF DOOR
CLOSED

PIANO
HINGE

TOP
SECTION
DETAIL.

1 X 4

#96

⅛"

PLASTIC LAMINATE (FORMICA)
(OPTIONAL)

30°

TO AVOID DRILLING
TOO FAR, MARK THE DRILL
BIT WITH TAPE AT THE
CORRECT DEPTH.

SCRAP
2 X 4
CUT AT
30°

#97

Cut dozens of 2 in. long pegs from a 3/8 in. dowel, keeping those you don't use in a jar for future use. Spread some white glue in the holes and hammer in the pegs where you want them. You have three choices for showing where your tools belong in the tool chest: (1) Outline the tool on the backboard and paint in the silhouette (a steady hand is required); (2) cut the tool profile out of contact paper and press on after first sanding and varnishing the underlying surface; or (3) label the position of the tool with a labeling gun. Certain tools like drills, screwdrivers, chisels, and files are difficult to hang on pegs and require a different solution. For some ideas, see illus. #98.

Many years ago some clever person discovered that hanging glass jars to the underside of a shelf was a good way to store screws, nuts, and bolts (see illus. #99). The only difficulty is finding enough jars of the same size. Baby-food jars or small mayonnaise jars seem to work well, but who can eat eighteen jars of mayonnaise? It's almost

worth it to buy new Mason jars all the same size.

To keep the tools in place, make a wooden crossbar from a piece of scrap wood and an old thread spool and screw it to the back board (see illus. #100).

To store sandpaper, make a folder out of cardboard. Provide two sections, one for coarse sandpaper and one for fine (see illus. #101).

Finish by covering the wood with three coats of polyurethane.

To hang the tool chest on the wall, first locate the two 2 x 4 wood studs behind the wall (see page 00). Bore 1/2 in. diameter holes in each one about 5-1/2 ft. above the floor. Make sure they are level and at the same angle. Drive a 1/2 in. wood dowel into each hole. Bore two larger 3/4 in. diameter holes in the back of the cabinet at the corresponding width and hang the tool chest onto the pegs. As a safeguard against falling, nail a 1 x 2 support to the wall under the tool chest.

TOOL CHEST

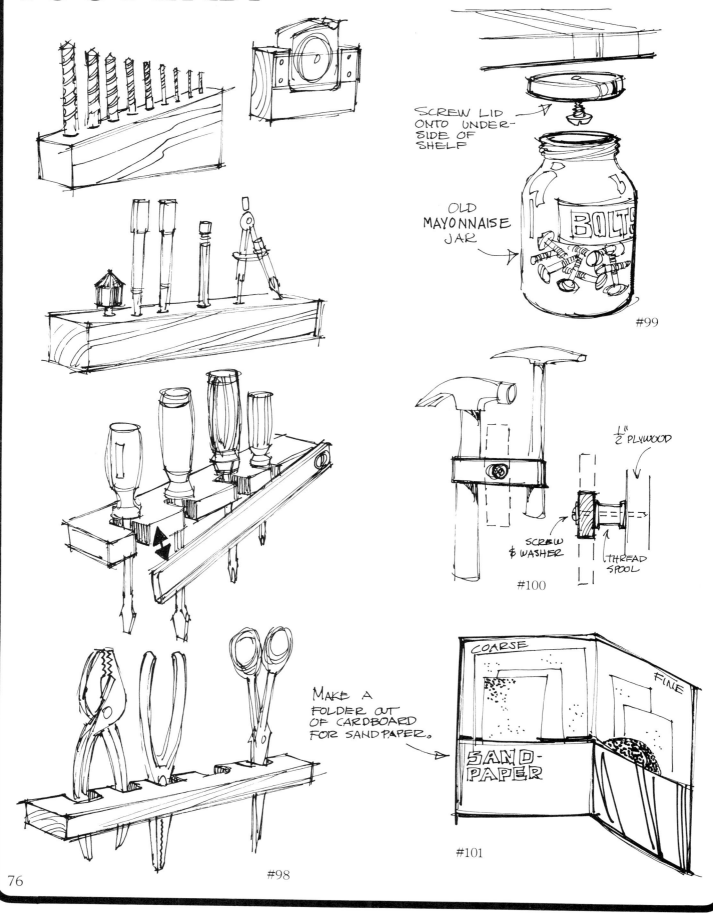

SCREW LID ONTO UNDER-SIDE OF SHELF

OLD MAYONNAISE JAR

BOLTS

#99

1/2" PLYWOOD

SCREW & WASHER

THREAD SPOOL

#100

MAKE A FOLDER OUT OF CARDBOARD FOR SANDPAPER.

COARSE

FINE

SAND-PAPER

#101

#98

CHILD'S ART DESK

CHILD'S ART DESK

Psychologists and educators are becoming increasingly aware that artistic development doesn't simply help the child to become an "artist"; it also helps the child in his or her understanding and interpretation of reality and the surrounding world. Drawing and painting also aid a child in the coordination and development of small motor skills and are a learning tool in discovering colors, shapes, and textures.

Besides being a valuable asset to the child's intellectual growth, the art desk is also useful in providing many hours of quiet time during which the parents can get some of their own work done.

One of the features of the art desk is the practically endless roll of drawing paper which fits through a slot at the top and under a tear-off bar at the bottom of the drawing board. When the child is finished with drawing, he or she can tear it off by slipping the paper down under the bar and pulling. There's no need to call Mom or Dad. The paper tear-off bar also prevents crayons, pencils, or scissors from sliding off the board.

The front compartment holds small poster paint bottles, paste, scissors, crayons, or whatever the child chooses in the way of art materials, while the rear compartment stores items not so often used—markers, various sized brushes, colored pencils—all neatly stored in plastic flowerpots bought at your local variety store.

Where do you keep a child's finished art work after it has been admired and shown to friends and relatives? In the child's art desk, of course, under the lift-up desk top. As the drawings begin to accumulate, the child can be encouraged to clean out the desk—a chore many adults have difficulty in doing—and throw away old drawings to make room for the new.

A worthwhile investment is a small clamp lamp with a 75 watt bulb so you can be sure your child has plenty of light to work by.

As your child grows taller, the art desk can be adjusted to accommodate his or her larger size by removing the four bolts on the side, lifting the table up until the next set of holes lines up, and inserting the bolts in their new location. Note that the three sets of holes are in the side of the desk itself, not in the two supporting vertical columns.

How to Make the Child's Art Desk

The art desk is fairly easy to make and shouldn't take you more than one weekend plus a couple of evening hours. Here are the materials you'll need:

Two 2 x 4s, 24 in. long
Two 5/4 in. x 8 in., 22 in. long
(You may not be familiar with 5/4 lumber, but most lumberyards carry it. It's slightly thicker than 1 in.)
One 3/4 in. birch plywood, 36 x 26 in.
One 1/2 in. A/C plywood, 48 x 24 in.
One 1/2 in. dowel, 36 in. long
One 1 in. aluminum flat stock, 24 in. long
Four 3 x 3/8 in. carriage bolts
Plastic laminate
    desk top 24 x 16 in.
    front compartment 1-1/2 x 22-1/2 in.
    2-1/2 x 22-1/2 in.
    sides 15 x 26 in.

Note: If you are buying the plastic laminate in small sizes, it will improve the appearance if you use a bright solid color for the sides and front.

Begin construction by cutting out the sides (see side view, illus. #103) according to the dimensions shown in the plan. Drill 1/2 in. holes for the hinge.

Cut out the 1/2 in. thick plywood top and notch the top corners as shown (see illus. #104). Flatten one side of the 1/2 in. diameter dowel (leaving 3/4 in. on the ends round). Glue and nail the dowel to the top edge of the desk top. Apply the plastic laminate with the straightest edge at the top. (It will be impossible to trim this later). Round off the edges slightly, sanding them smooth.

While the glue on the hinge is drying, cut the front compartment pieces, the paper roll holder, and the rear compartment pieces all the exact same length (22-1/2 in.). Round

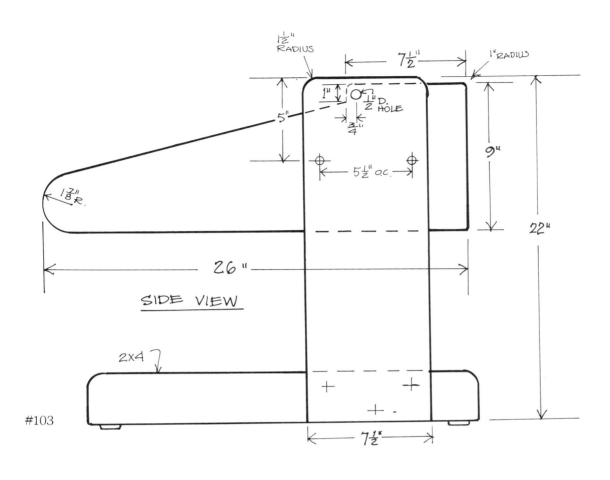

SIDE VIEW

1½" RADIUS

1" RADIUS

7½"

1" D. HOLE

3/4"

5"

9"

22"

5½" O.C.

1 7/8" R.

26"

2x4

#103

7½"

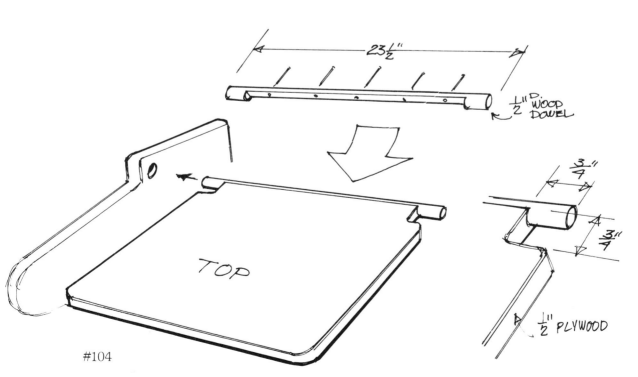

23½"

½" D. WOOD DOWEL

3/4"

3/4"

TOP

½" PLYWOOD

#104

CHILD'S ART DESK

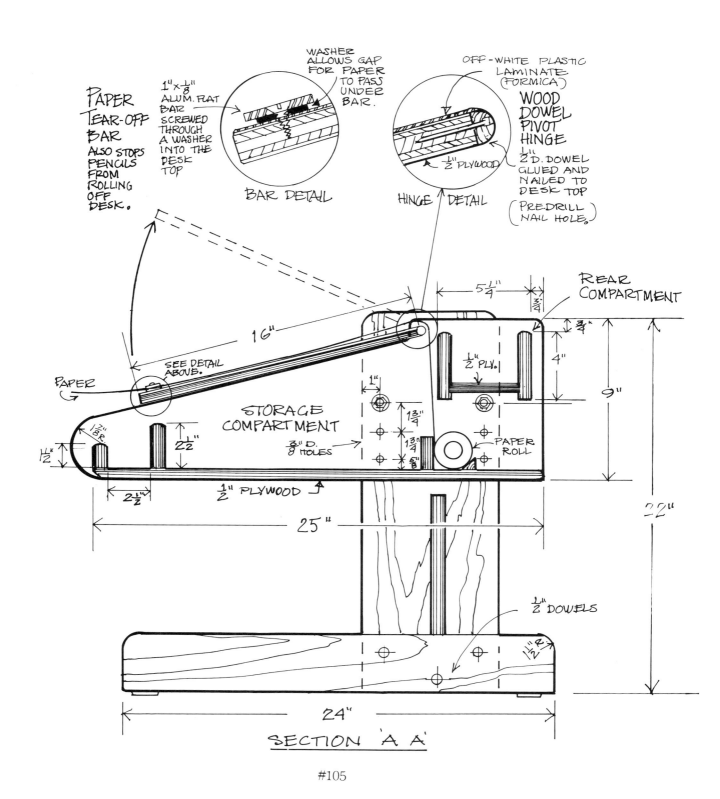

PAPER
TEAR-OFF
BAR
ALSO STOPS
PENCILS
FROM
ROLLING
OFF
DESK.

1"×1/8" ALUM. FLAT BAR SCREWED THROUGH A WASHER INTO THE DESK TOP

WASHER ALLOWS GAP FOR PAPER TO PASS UNDER BAR.

BAR DETAIL

OFF-WHITE PLASTIC LAMINATE (FORMICA)

WOOD DOWEL PIVOT HINGE

1/2" PLYWOOD

HINGE DETAIL

1" D. DOWEL GLUED AND NAILED TO DESK TOP (PREDRILL NAIL HOLE.)

REAR COMPARTMENT

5 1/4"

3/4"

3/4"

4"

9"

1/2" PLY.

16"

SEE DETAIL ABOVE.

PAPER

1"

STORAGE COMPARTMENT

1 3/4"

1 3/4"

5/8"

PAPER ROLL

3/4" D. 8 HOLES

1 3/8" R

2 1/2"

1 1/2"

1/2" PLYWOOD

2 1/2"

25"

22"

1/2" DOWELS

1 1/2" R

24"

SECTION 'A A'

#105

80

CHILD'S ART DESK

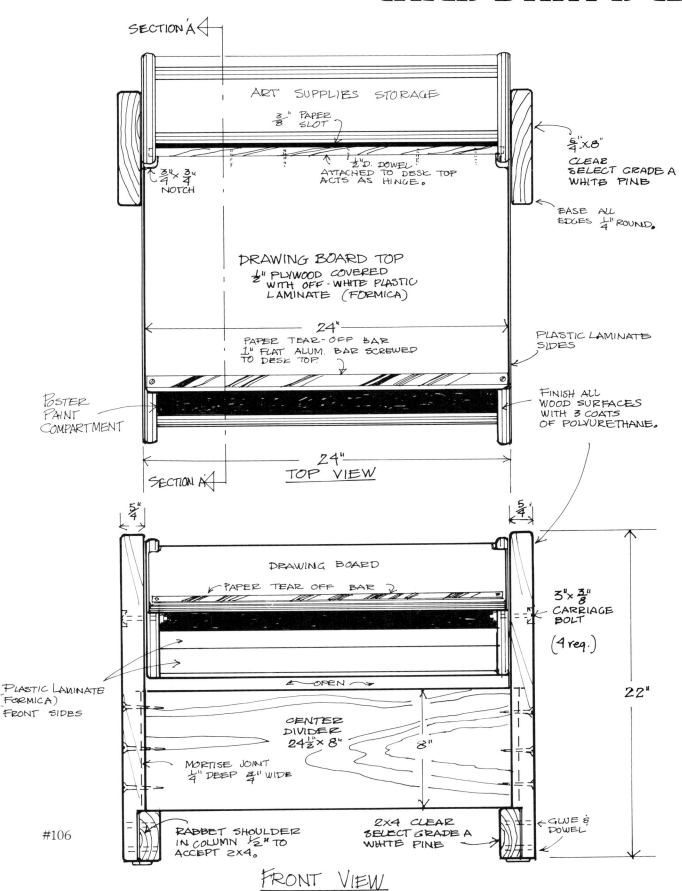

SECTION 'A'

ART SUPPLIES STORAGE

$\frac{3}{8}$" PAPER SLOT

$\frac{1}{2}$"D. DOWEL ATTACHED TO DESK TOP ACTS AS HINGE.

$\frac{3}{4}$" x $\frac{3}{4}$" NOTCH

$\frac{5}{4}$" x 8" CLEAR SELECT GRADE A WHITE PINE

EASE ALL EDGES $\frac{1}{4}$" ROUND.

DRAWING BOARD TOP
$\frac{1}{2}$" PLYWOOD COVERED WITH OFF-WHITE PLASTIC LAMINATE (FORMICA)

24"

PAPER TEAR-OFF BAR
1" FLAT ALUM. BAR SCREWED TO DESK TOP.

PLASTIC LAMINATE SIDES

POSTER PAINT COMPARTMENT

FINISH ALL WOOD SURFACES WITH 3 COATS OF POLYURETHANE.

24"

SECTION 'A'

TOP VIEW

$\frac{5}{4}$"

$\frac{5}{4}$"

DRAWING BOARD

PAPER TEAR OFF BAR

3" x $\frac{3}{8}$" CARRIAGE BOLT

(4 req.)

22"

PLASTIC LAMINATE (FORMICA) FRONT SIDES

OPEN

CENTER DIVIDER
$24\frac{1}{2}$" x 8"

8"

MORTISE JOINT $\frac{1}{4}$" DEEP $\frac{3}{4}$" WIDE

#106

RABBET SHOULDER IN COLUMN $\frac{1}{2}$" TO ACCEPT 2x4.

2x4 CLEAR SELECT GRADE A WHITE PINE

GLUE & DOWEL

FRONT VIEW

off the top edges and sand smooth. Nail and glue the rear compartment together. Cut the bottom from 1/2 in. plywood, place it on a flat table, and stand the two sides next to it. Carefully glue and nail the sides to the bottom. Now mark and place each cross piece in position, making sure the desk top is in place first. Glue and nail all the cross pieces, check for squareness, and set aside to dry.

The pedestal that holds the art desk is made up of two feet, two columns, and a cross divider connecting the two. Cut and sand all the pieces. Mark the center of the inside of the columns and chisel out a 3/4 in. wide, 1/2 in. deep dado groove to accept the center divider. Cut a notch in the bottom of the column for the 2 x 4s by making a cut across the grain at the height of the 2 x 4s and then splitting out the wood with a hammer and chisel. Finish off the joint with a rasp. Place the 2 x 4s in position and either screw or dowel them in place. Glue and screw the columns onto the divider using 2-1/2 in. long #10 flathead screws. Check for squareness and check to see if the desk fits into the pedestal perfectly.

Put the pedestal aside to dry, and apply plastic laminate to the sides of the desk. Round off all edges and sand smooth. Apply plastic laminate to the two front pieces, and cut it to the exact dimensions, testing it for correct size before applying the adhesive.

Screw the aluminum bar on the lower edge of the desk, making sure to place a washer under each end in order to provide a gap for the paper.

Carefully mark and drill the top pair of 3/8 in. holes for the bolts on each side. Lay the pedestal on its side and place the art desk on the pedestal, marking where the holes correspond on the columns. Drill the holes in the columns. Measure down 1-3/4 in. from the first bolt holes drilled in the side of the art desk and drill a new set of holes exactly the same distance apart. Repeat.

Give all the bare wood surfaces three coats of polyurethane and allow to dry. Assemble the art desk on the lowest level if your child is a 2-year-old; increase the height for every two additional years.

You will notice that all the surfaces that are likely to get the most paint, dirt, and wear are protected by plastic laminate. If the surfaces do get paint on them, you can easily clean them by wiping with a soft sponge and cleanser (Fantastic works well). Even marker pen accidents come off plastic laminate if you use the right cleanser (Flo Master cleanser made by Venus Esterbrook, sold in art, drafting supply, and stationery stores).

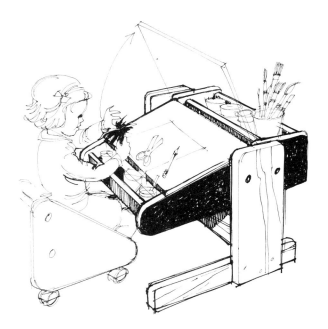

KITCHEN/WORKBENCH

KITCHEN/WORKBENCH

All children love to play with water, and a functioning kitchen sink is a great way for them to enjoy this activity. This kitchen is on casters and can be rolled from room to room. It has its own plumbing system (a pump and a water reservoir with a drain). The plastic porta-sink can be bought at most camping stores and the plastic surface is easily cleaned with soap and water. Most camping stores carry a heavy-duty, inexpensive (approximately $12) set of pots, pans, dishes, and utensils. The burners for the "pretend" cooking range, the knobs, and the clock are all make-ups. This piece of play equipment has kept our 4-year-old and her friends busy for many an hour. When

our daughter outgrows it, we plan to convert it into a workbench.

A workbench is one of the best early toys to develop a child's building skills. By imitating, the child soon learns the satisfaction of creating and building projects out of wood. For the surface of the workbench, use a sheet of 1/8 in. thick hardboard (Masonite) (see illus. #107). A simple rack can be made for small tools by boring holes in a 2 x 4 and screwing it into the back support, while larger tools fit easily into the two drawers underneath. Saws rest easily on wooden dowels placed on the side of the workbench out of harm's way (see illus. #109).

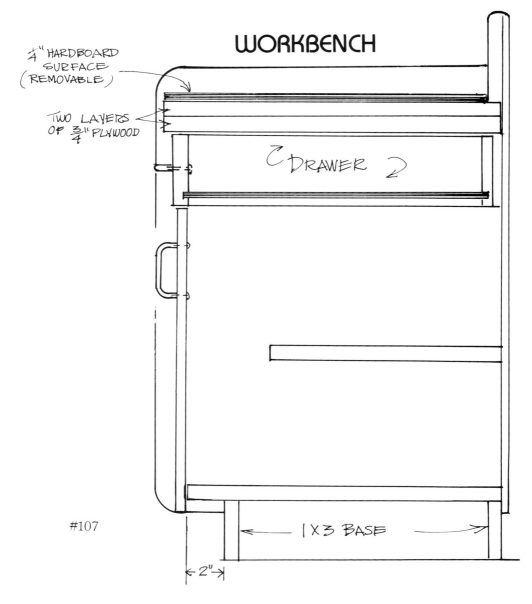

WORKBENCH

1/4" HARDBOARD SURFACE (REMOVABLE)

TWO LAYERS OF 3/4" PLYWOOD

DRAWER

#107

1 X 3 BASE

2"

KITCHEN/WORKBENCH

KITCHEN

#108

WORKBENCH—
SAME BASIC PLANS AS KITCHEN

#109

KITCHEN/WORKBENCH

How to Make the Kitchen/Workbench

The procedure is very similar whether you are making the kitchen or the workbench. Begin by cutting all the pieces out of 3/4 in. thick plywood. Since most of the pieces will be covered with plastic laminate, average grade plywood is adequate. Only the front should be high grade birch.

If you are making the workbench, cut an extra piece 17-3/4 x 31 in. and glue and nail it to the other top piece to make a 1-1/2 in. thick, strong top.

Glue a 1-1/2 in. plastic laminate face strip to the front edge of the top surface and trim it flush. Glue plastic laminate onto the top surface, overlapping the face strip, and trim off all sides square. Trace the outline of the sink with a pencil and cut it out with a saber saw. It's important to do these steps now, as it's almost impossible to do them later.

For the workbench, leave the top surface wood; however, to protect it from airplane glue, paint, etc., use a removable piece of 1/4 in. hardboard cut to the same size as the surface of the bench. This can be discarded when it becomes too scratched and a new one slipped into place.

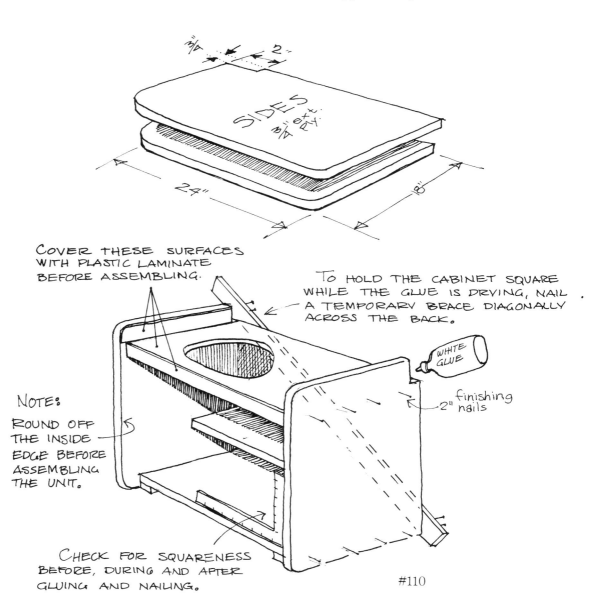

COVER THESE SURFACES WITH PLASTIC LAMINATE BEFORE ASSEMBLING.

To HOLD THE CABINET SQUARE WHILE THE GLUE IS DRYING, NAIL A TEMPORARY BRACE DIAGONALLY ACROSS THE BACK.

WHITE GLUE

2" finishing nails

NOTE:

ROUND OFF THE INSIDE EDGE BEFORE ASSEMBLING THE UNIT.

CHECK FOR SQUARENESS BEFORE, DURING AND AFTER GLUING AND NAILING.

#110

Glue and nail the sides to the top front two shelves. After making sure it is square, nail a temporary diagonal board across the back to hold it in place while it's drying (see illus. #110). Cut the back out of 1/4 in. hardboard (Masonite). Glue and nail it to the back. The backsplash is then glued and screwed to the sides. Be sure to first glue plastic laminate to the front surface (kitchen only). Use glue and clamps to hold the backsplash to the hardboard (Masonite) back panel. Round the edges when the glue dries to hide the back panel as much as possible (see illus. #112).

Glue and nail the front panel under the counter, first covering the front face with plastic laminate. On the workbench the 4 in. space under the 1-1/2 in. thick top is used for two tool drawers. To make the drawers see pages 13 – 17.

Cover the sides with plastic laminate, making sure to overlap the hardwood back.

Round the edges and sand smooth (see pages 6–9). Cut the door panels out of 1/2 in. birch plywood 16-1/2 x 15-1/2 in. and attach them to the sides with piano hinges (see illus. #113). Add four casters to the bottom and finish with three coats of polyurethane.

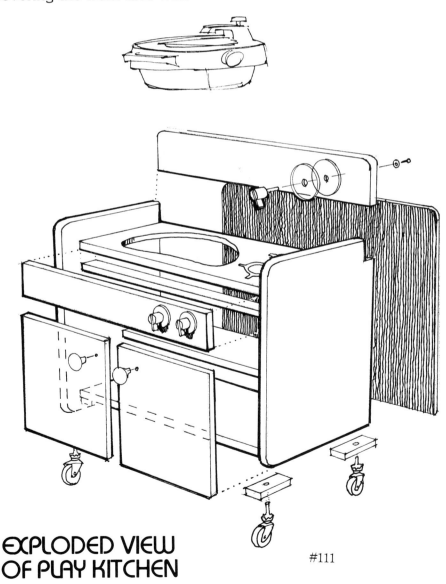

EXPLODED VIEW
OF PLAY KITCHEN

#111

KITCHEN/WORKBENCH

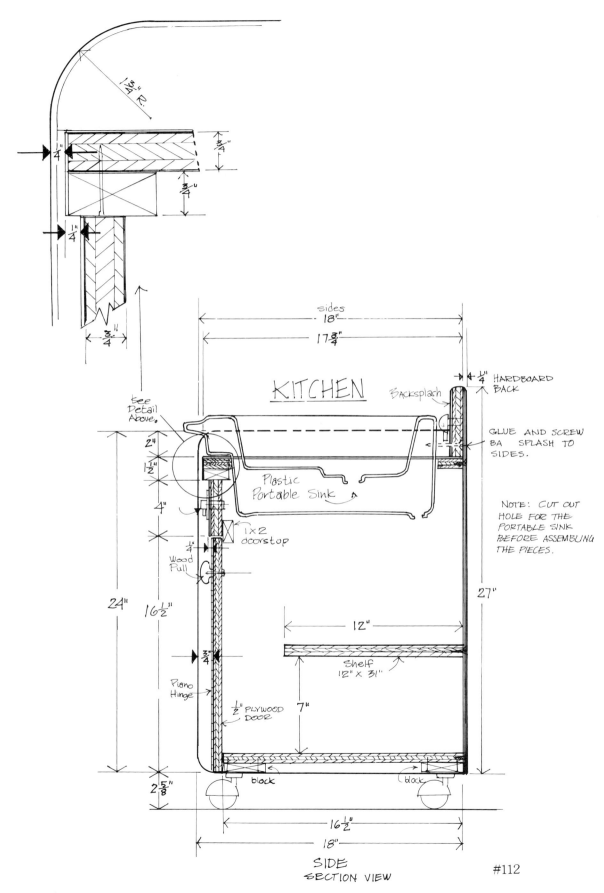

$1\frac{3}{4}"$ R.

$\frac{3}{4}"$

$\frac{1}{4}"$

$\frac{3}{4}"$

$\frac{1}{4}"$

$\frac{3}{4}"$

sides
18"

$17\frac{3}{4}"$

KITCHEN

Backsplash

$\frac{1}{4}"$ HARDBOARD BACK

GLUE AND SCREW BA SPLASH TO SIDES.

NOTE: CUT OUT HOLE FOR THE PORTABLE SINK BEFORE ASSEMBLING THE PIECES.

See Detail Above.

2"

$1\frac{1}{2}"$

Plastic Portable Sink

4"

$\frac{1}{4}"$

1×2 doorstop

Wood Pull

24"

$16\frac{1}{2}"$

27"

12"

$\frac{3}{4}"$

Shelf
12" X 31"

Piano Hinge

$\frac{1}{2}"$ PLYWOOD DOOR

7"

$2\frac{5}{8}"$

block

block

$16\frac{1}{2}"$

18"

SIDE
SECTION VIEW

#112

ATTACHING THE DOORS

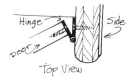

Hinge — Door — Side

Top View

TO ATTACH THE DOORS, CUT TWO PIECES OF PIANO HINGE 16½" LONG. SCREW ALL THE SCREWS INTO THE DOOR FIRST.

MOUNT THE DOOR TO THE INSIDE WALL OF THE CABINET BY STARTING ONE SCREW AT THE TOP FIRST, AND THEN ONE AT THE BOTTOM. CHECK THE ALIGNMENT BEFORE PROCEEDING ANY FURTHER.

IT IS SIMPLER AND FASTER TO DRILL A PILOT HOLE SLIGHTLY SMALLER THAN THE SCREW ITSELF, BEFORE ATTEMPTING TO PUT THE SCREW IN.

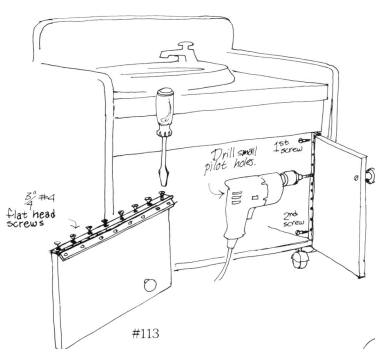

Drill small pilot holes.

1st screw

2nd screw

3/4" #4 flat head screws

#113

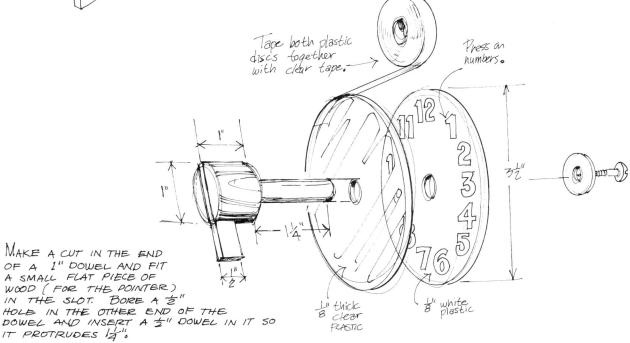

Tape both plastic discs together with clear tape.

Press on numbers.

3½"

1"

1"

1¼"

½"

MAKE A CUT IN THE END OF A 1" DOWEL AND FIT A SMALL FLAT PIECE OF WOOD (FOR THE POINTER) IN THE SLOT. BORE A ½" HOLE IN THE OTHER END OF THE DOWEL AND INSERT A ½" DOWEL IN IT SO IT PROTRUDES 1¼".

CUT TWO DISCS FROM ⅛" THICK PLASTIC (AS SHOWN), ADD NUMBERS AND DRILL A ½" HOLE IN THE CENTER. DRILL AN IDENTICAL ½" DIA. HOLE IN THE BACKSPLASH AND PUSH THE ASSEMBLY TOGETHER.

⅛" thick clear plastic

⅛" white plastic

#114

KITCHEN/WORKBENCH

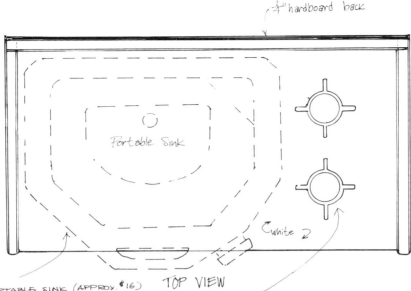

¼" hardboard back

Portable Sink

white

TOP VIEW

BUY A PLASTIC PORTABLE SINK (APPROX. $16)
FROM A NAUTICAL OR CAMPING SUPPLY
OUTLET. TRACE AROUND IT WITH A PENCIL
AND CUT AN OPENING FOR THE SINK TO
FIT INTO.

BURNERS ARE MADE BY CUTTING A MASK OUT OF
CONTACT PAPER, PRESSING IT ONTO THE COUNTER
SURFACE, AND SPRAYING IT WITH ENAMEL.
FOR A MORE PERMANENT JOB, CUT A ⅛" DEEP
GROOVE WITH A ROUTER AND FILL THE RECESS
WITH GREY EPOXY PASTE.

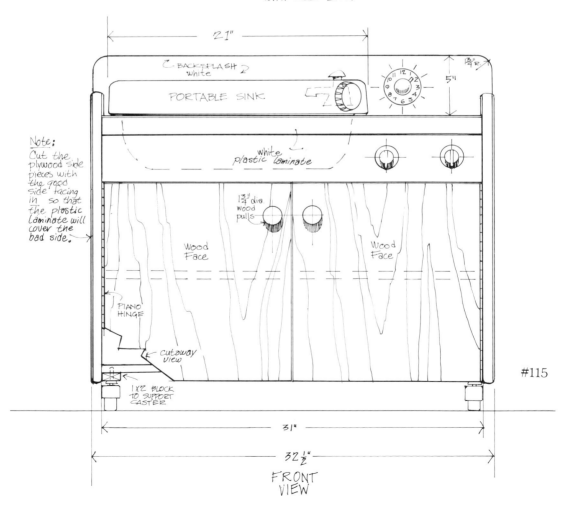

21"

BACKSPLASH
white

PORTABLE SINK

5"

1¾" R.

Note:
Cut the
plywood side
pieces with
the good
side facing
in so that
the plastic
laminate will
cover the
bad side.

white
plastic laminate

1¾" dia.
wood
pulls

Wood
Face

Wood
Face

PIANO
HINGE

cutaway
view

1×2 BLOCK
TO SUPPORT
CASTER

#115

31"

32½"

FRONT
VIEW

TRICYCLE

PLAY

TRICYCLE

You may be aware of a toy on the market called Big Wheels which is very popular with the 2-to-4-year-old set. It costs approximately $20, is made of cheap plastic, and makes a horrible noise (which probably accounts for its popularity). This wood tricycle could be your competitor to Big Wheels.

This project received more enthusiastic attention from my daughter than any other project in this book. The tricycle is easy to make and only took one afternoon to construct. The whole tricycle can be cut out of a small 14 x 22 in. piece of scrap plywood and requires only a jigsaw, hammer, and drill for tools. However, you'll have to make a trip to the hardware store to buy a 3 in. diameter white plastic caster, two 1/4 x 2 in. carriage bolts, five 2 in. flathead screws, and a 1 in. diameter wood dowel for the axle and handle.

This tricycle was intended for 2-year-old toddlers to help them strengthen their leg muscles. Children love anything that moves them from one place to another. It's not surprising that young children like any mobile object. After all, they only just emerged from the womb, the crib, and the infant seat. No wonder they want to explore the world at maximum speed.

How to Make the Tricycle

With a pencil and ruler lay out the shapes onto a 3/4 in. thick piece of plywood and cut them out with an electric saber saw, a coping saw, or a jigsaw.

Drill out 1 in. diameter holes for the handle and the axle.

Assemble all the parts with glue and screws and be sure to countersink the screws below the surface of the plywood.

Flatten one side of the 1 in. axle dowel where it rests against the back, and bolt it to the back with 1/4 x 2 in. carriage bolts.

Attach the wheels. Drill a 1/4 in. hole in the ends of the axle and insert a peg to secure the wheel.

Drill a hole for the caster. Don't use the metal clip that fits around the caster. Remove it and use only the bare shank. Fill the hole with plastic wood, insert the shank of the caster, and allow it to dry.

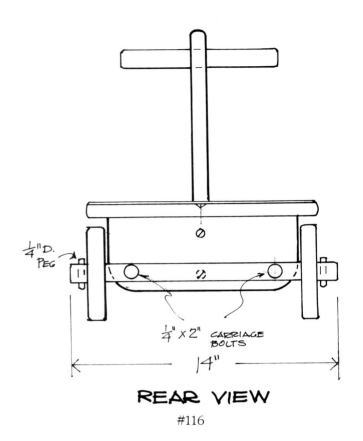

1/4" D. PEG

1/4" X 2" CARRIAGE BOLTS

14"

REAR VIEW

#116

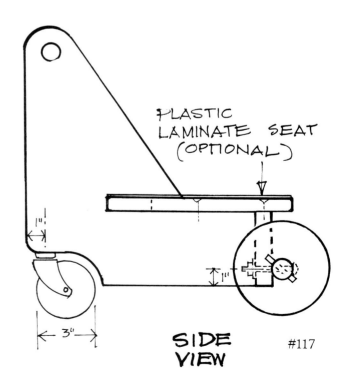

PLASTIC LAMINATE SEAT (OPTIONAL)

1"

1"

3"

SIDE VIEW

#117

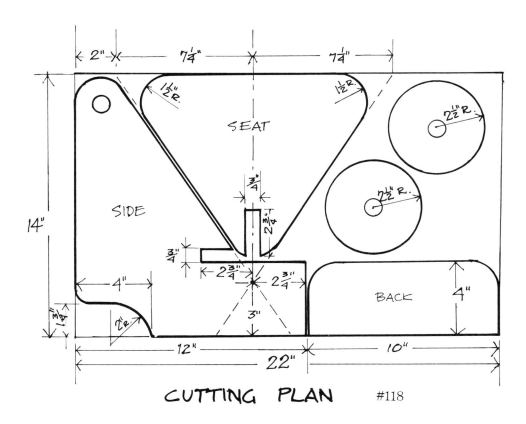

CUTTING PLAN   #118

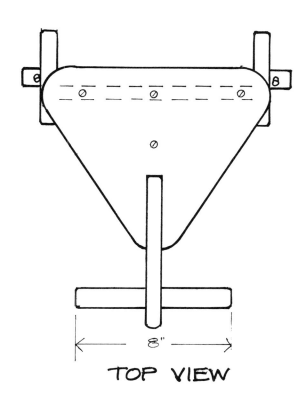

TOP VIEW

Fill all holes with wood putty and sand all the edges smooth so that there is no possibility of the child getting a splinter from the plywood.

Leave the wood bare but cover the seat and handles with several coats of varnish or polyurethane.

PLAY HOUSE

PLAY HOUSE

- Each side provides a different situation for role playing.
- Stores flat when not in use.
- Rope corners provide a safety edge.
- Can be assembled by the child to give a sense of creating his or her own environment.

Instead of building a separate play house for each fantasy situation, try building one with four different sides. When the children become tired of playing "fireman," they can move to another side and play "store," then "magic theater," and then "mailman." This is an excellent indoor occupation for children during rainy days or the cold winter months, and the structure can easily be dismantled and stored flat in the summer to allow for more room.

How to Make the Play House

Buy two 4 ft. x 8 ft. x 1/4 in. thick *tempered* Masonite. Be sure it is tempered: tempered Masonite is very dark brown and smooth on both sides.

Cut out four rectangular panels 48 x 42 in. Stack them together like a sandwich and hold them with several clamps. Round off the corners by cutting a 5-1/2 in. radius with a saber saw. While all four pieces are still together, bore 3/4 in. holes, 6 in. apart, 1-1/2

in. in from the side edges (to accept the ropes later on; see illus. #119). Cut the openings with a saber saw according to the plan (illus. #120).

Paint the outside surfaces with a shellac-base white sealer. You will need denatured alcohol to clean your brush or roller. This type of sealer dries quickly and seeps into the Masonite, leaving a flat smooth surface.

Buy four spray cans of colored enamel and spray each side a different color. Using spray paint eliminates the messy bother of cleaning the brush four times and let's you do a much more professional-looking job. In addition, spray paint usually dries within minutes, whereas some brush-on enamels can take days to dry, even though the label says "quick drying."

Before spraying, check the surface to be sure it is free of dust or blemishes and mask the sides where the holes are with 2 in. masking tape (the rope that holds the corners together would eventually mar the paint if this area were painted).

Use your imagination in decorating the sides. Bear in mind that it's very difficult to paint a straight freehand line with a brush. The best way is to buy a few yards of clear contact paper, remove the protective backing, and press it down lightly where you want your graphics. Sketch your graphics with a marker pen directly onto the contact paper and then cut out the letters with an Exacto or matte knife. It is unnecessary to rub down the contact paper, as this will be removed later. Choose an accent color for the graphics. These colors are often found where they sell spray touch-up colors in small cans for cars. Spray the cut-out portion with the accent color, making sure that you have first covered the entire surrounding area with newspaper to catch any overspray. For smaller lettering, use rub-on, pressure-sensitive letters.

Construct the shelves or storage ledge with scrap plywood, making sure to sand all edges smooth, then paint with three or four coats of polyurethane (illus. #121).

The curtains for the theater can be made with any leftover fabric. We used velvet, which looks great.

If you have any leftover scraps of plastic laminate, cut them out and contact-cement them onto the surface for decoration. This is actually easier to do than freehand painting, and the results are far superior, as it never needs to be retouched.

Lace a 1/2 in. polypropylene rope (you'll need 50 ft.) up the sides, over the top, and down the opposite corners. The crossing of ropes at the top adds strength to the cube. It also forms an X for a roof, from which stage sets can be hung using clothespins or large clips.

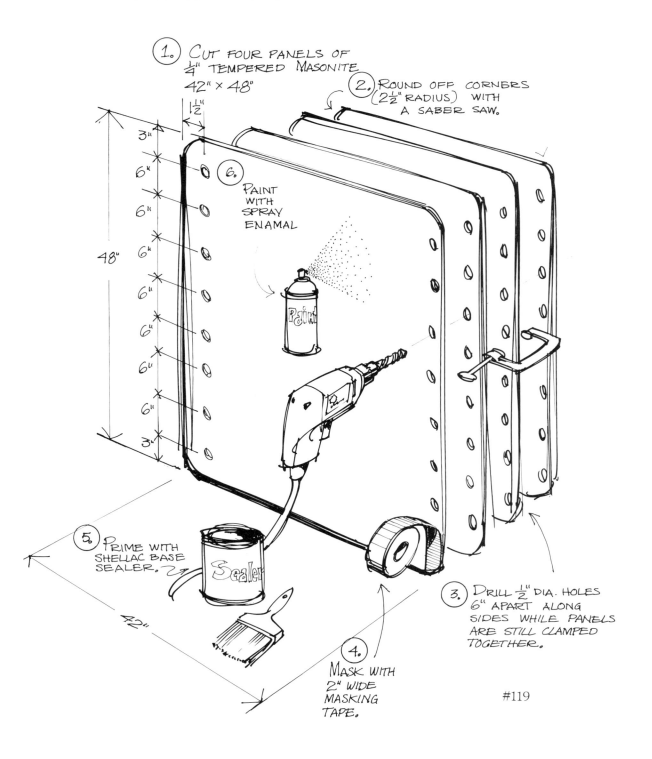

1. CUT FOUR PANELS OF 1/4" TEMPERED MASONITE 42" × 48"

2. ROUND OFF CORNERS (2½" RADIUS) WITH A SABER SAW.

6. PAINT WITH SPRAY ENAMAL

1½"
3"
6"
6"
6"
48" 6"
6"
6"
6"
3"

5. PRIME WITH SHELLAC BASE SEALER.

Sealer

42"

4. MASK WITH 2" WIDE MASKING TAPE.

3. DRILL ½" DIA. HOLES 6" APART ALONG SIDES WHILE PANELS ARE STILL CLAMPED TOGETHER.

#119

97

PLAY HOUSE

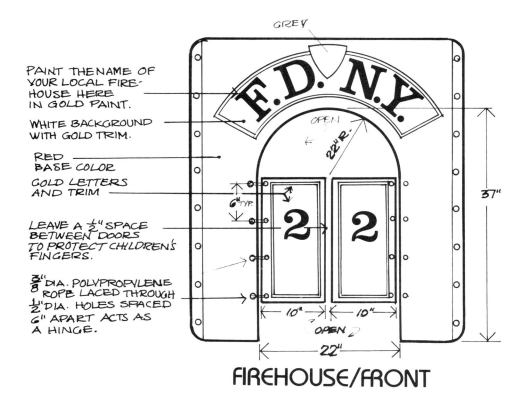

GREY

PAINT THE NAME OF YOUR LOCAL FIRE-HOUSE HERE IN GOLD PAINT.

WHITE BACKGROUND WITH GOLD TRIM.

RED BASE COLOR

GOLD LETTERS AND TRIM

LEAVE A $\frac{1}{2}$" SPACE BETWEEN DOORS TO PROTECT CHILDREN'S FINGERS.

$\frac{3}{8}$" DIA. POLYPROPYLENE ROPE LACED THROUGH $\frac{1}{2}$" DIA. HOLES SPACED 6" APART ACTS AS A HINGE.

F.D. N.Y.

OPEN

22"R.

2   2

6" TYP.

37"

10"   10"

OPEN

22"

FIREHOUSE/FRONT

#120

1X2 VERTICAL GUIDES WITH $\frac{1}{4}$" DADO GROOVES ARE MOUNTED INSIDE TO HOLD GRILLE

$\frac{1}{4}$"

WHITE SIGN WITH BLACK LETTERS

BLUE BASE COLOR

LEFTOVER SCRAP FROM CUT-OUT USED AS GRILLE.

POST OFFICE

CUT-OUT SLOT FOR LETTERS

17"

10"

OPEN   2"

BLOCKS STOP GRILLE FROM DESCENDING THE LAST 2"

GRILLE

BORE 1" HOLES TOP AND BOTTOM AND CUT OUT SPACES BETWEEN BARS WITH A SABER SAW.

SHELF

SEE DETAILS

RED STAR ON WHITE BACKGROUND

22"

15"

POST OFFICE/RIGHT SIDE

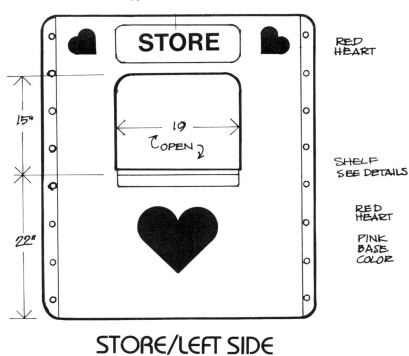

WHITE SIGN
BLACK LETTERS

STORE

RED
HEART

15"

19
OPEN

22"

RED
HEART

SHELF
SEE DETAILS

RED
HEART

PINK
BASE
COLOR

STORE/LEFT SIDE

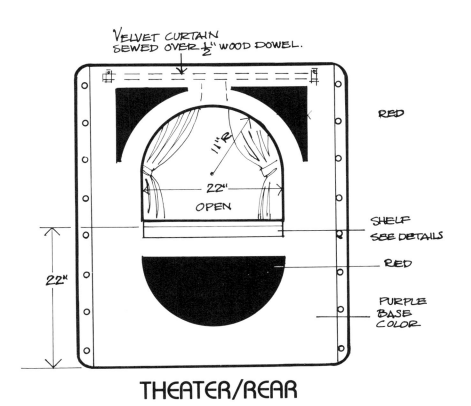

VELVET CURTAIN
SEWED OVER ½" WOOD DOWEL.

RED

11"R

22"
OPEN

SHELF
SEE DETAILS

RED

22"

PURPLE
BASE
COLOR

THEATER/REAR

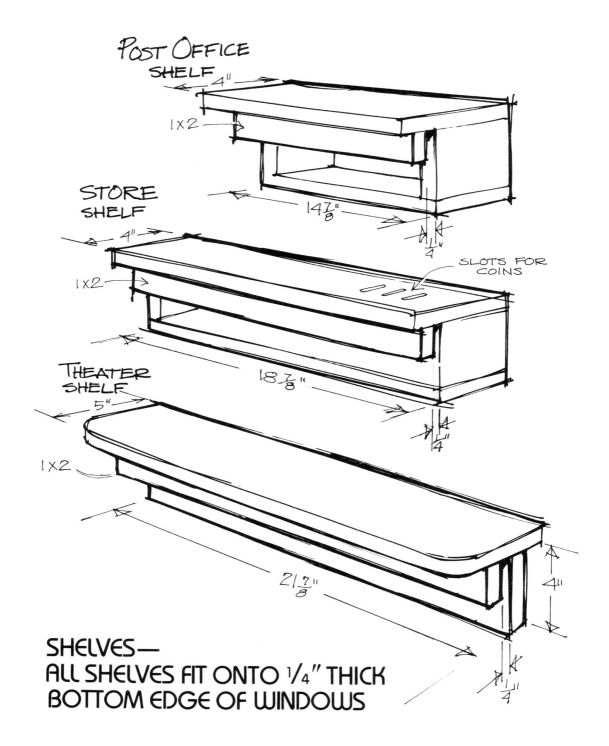

Post Office
SHELF
4"
1X2
14 7/8"
1/4"

STORE
SHELF
4"
1X2
SLOTS FOR COINS
18 7/8"
1/4"

THEATER
SHELF
5"
1X2
21 7/8"
4"
1/4"

SHELVES—
ALL SHELVES FIT ONTO 1/4" THICK
BOTTOM EDGE OF WINDOWS

#121

TOY STORAGE UNIT

STORAGE

TOY STORAGE UNIT

The toy storage unit has a long and useful life — beginning with storing a 2-year-old's dolls, costumes, pull toys, or out-of-season clothes. As the child grows older it can be filled with larger toys and records; it can be used to store sporting equipment; and when the child begins school it can become a filing cabinet, which can last almost indefinitely.

If in later life the colors of plastic laminate used are too reminiscent of childhood days, a new layer of plastic laminate can be applied right over the old. This is done by sanding the old surface with very coarse sandpaper, bringing up a "tooth" to which the contact cement can adhere.

This is a simple design and should take you no more than one weekend.

How to Make the Toy Storage Unit

Cut all the cabinet pieces out of 3/4 in. birch plywood. Note that the side pieces overlap the back and bottom so the end grain will not show. Cut the top to the exact size and glue the plastic laminate to the top with contact cement. Round all the exposed edges with a router or file (see page 9) and sand smooth. Glue and nail the pieces together to form an open-ended box. Before hammering the nails all the way in, it's very important to make sure the sides are square with the bottom and top: this affects how the drawers will fit (see illus. #122). Finish the nailing by sinking the nail heads in 1/8 in. and filling the holes with wood putty. While the glue is still wet, make a final check to see that everything is square. Allow to dry for two hours.

This is a good time to cut all the pieces for the two drawers out of 1/2 in. birch plywood. Follow the plans shown in illus. #125. If, however, you don't have a tool to cut 1/4 in. dado grooves, refer to pages 14 – 15 for instructions on how to build simple drawers using butt joints. (There's nothing wrong with doing it that way — just be sure to change the measurements for the back and bottom.)

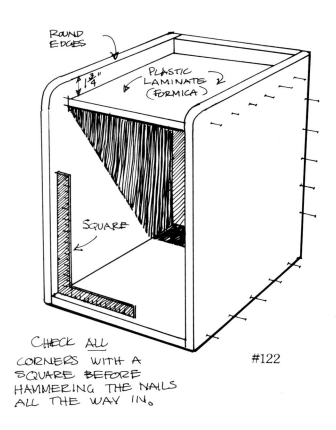

ROUND EDGES

1 3/4"

PLASTIC LAMINATE (FORMICA)

SQUARE

CHECK ALL CORNERS WITH A SQUARE BEFORE HAMMERING THE NAILS ALL THE WAY IN.

#122

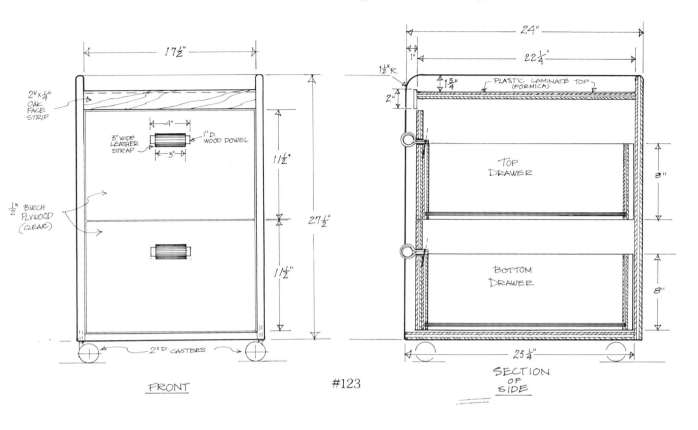

2" x 1/4"
OAK
FACE
STRIP

17 1/2"

3" WIDE
LEATHER
STRAP

4"

1" D.
WOOD DOWEL

3"

1/2" BIRCH
PLYWOOD
(CLEAR)

11 1/2"

27 1/2"

1 1/2"

2" D. CASTERS

FRONT

#123

24"

22 1/4"

1"

1 1/2" R.

1 3/4"

PLASTIC LAMINATE TOP
(FORMICA)

2"

TOP
DRAWER

8"

BOTTOM
DRAWER

8"

23 1/4"

SECTION
OF
SIDE

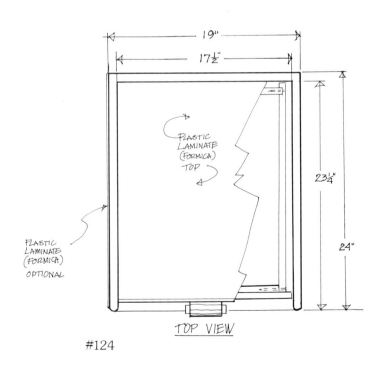

19"

17 1/2"

PLASTIC
LAMINATE
(FORMICA)
TOP

23 1/4"

24"

PLASTIC
LAMINATE
(FORMICA)

OPTIONAL

TOP VIEW

#124

103

TOY STORAGE UNIT

Construct the two drawers using 1-1/2 in. finishing nails and glue. After making sure both drawers are square, clamp and glue the front onto the false front of the drawer. Allow to dry overnight.

Use your imagination when making the handle. If you want to make the one shown here, cut a slot out of the front of the two drawers just above the false front, 4 in. wide and 1/2 in. high. Buy a leather strap 4 in. wide and 1/4 in. thick (sold at most craft stores). Make a loop around a 1 in. wooden dowel and slip it through the slot. Secure it on the inside by nailing down through the leather into the top of the false front.

Because these drawers are expected to take heavy loads, it's best to hang them on 18 in. metal telescoping slides. Directions for hanging these are on the package they come in and on page 17 of this book.

Because this piece of furniture becomes heavy when full of records, etc., it is best to put it on 2 in. diameter casters. You will be very happy you did this the first time a piece of paper falls behind it and you have to move it forward.

Give all exposed wood a final light sanding and finish with three coats of polyurethane.

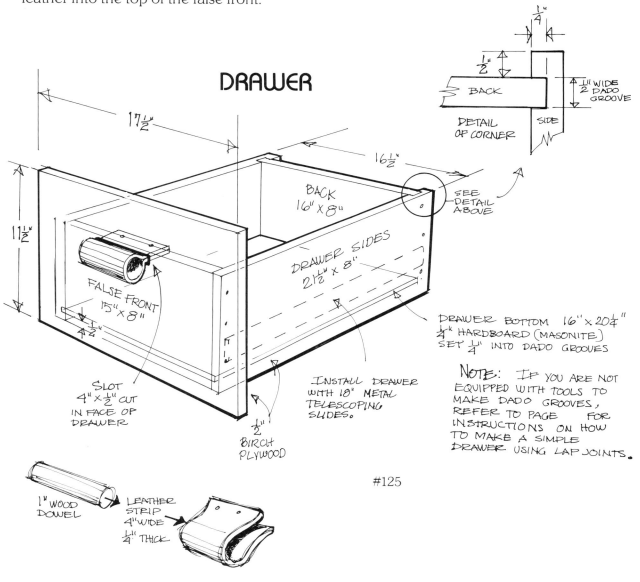

DRAWER

DETAIL OF CORNER

BACK

SIDE

$\frac{1}{4}$"

$\frac{1}{2}$"

$\frac{1}{2}$" WIDE DADO GROOVE

$17\frac{1}{2}$"

$16\frac{1}{2}$"

$11\frac{1}{2}$"

BACK 16" x 8"

SEE DETAIL ABOVE

DRAWER SIDES $2\frac{1}{2}$" x 8"

FALSE FRONT 15" x 8"

$\frac{1}{4}$" $\frac{1}{2}$"

SLOT 4" x $\frac{1}{2}$" CUT IN FACE OF DRAWER

$\frac{1}{2}$" BIRCH PLYWOOD

INSTALL DRAWER WITH 18" METAL TELESCOPING SLIDES.

DRAWER BOTTOM 16" x $20\frac{1}{4}$" $\frac{1}{4}$" HARDBOARD (MASONITE) SET $\frac{1}{4}$" INTO DADO GROOVES

NOTE: IF YOU ARE NOT EQUIPPED WITH TOOLS TO MAKE DADO GROOVES, REFER TO PAGE FOR INSTRUCTIONS ON HOW TO MAKE A SIMPLE DRAWER USING LAP JOINTS.

#125

1" WOOD DOWEL

LEATHER STRIP 4" WIDE $\frac{1}{4}$" THICK

PORTABLE STORAGE WAGON

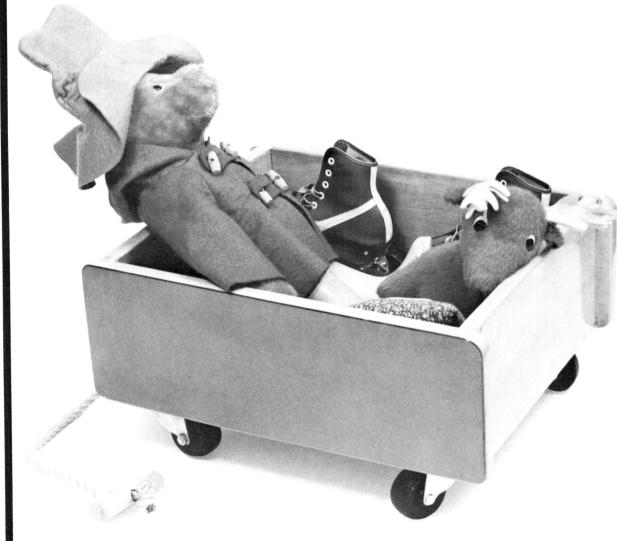

PORTABLE STORAGE WAGON

This storage wagon makes a great toy bin. For the child it is a push toy, a train, a car, a means of discovering locomotion. For the parent it is a storage place for the child's toys and a learning tool to help the child pick up toys. Cleaning up can actually be a happy time and source of accomplishment for the child when it is introduced as a game. This is a very useful toy to have around the house for the parents, since it's a dolly in disguise. If heavy-duty casters are used for wheels, very weighty objects can be moved by balancing them on top of the toy bin. Painting and cleaning supplies can be easily moved to different parts of the house as needed.

How to Make the Storage Wagon

Since this is basically a box on wheels (casters), it is one of the easiest projects in this book to make—a nice rainy-day job for Dad or Mom and a good project for the inexperienced. To keep it simple, I have eliminated difficult dado joints. You'll need a piece of 3/4 in. thick plywood. Cut exactly 18-1/2 x 14 in. for the bottom and a 3/4 x 7-1/2 in. board 6 ft. long for the sides and ends. You'll also need four 2-1/4 in. casters (plate type), a 1 in. dowel, 2 ft. of 3/8 in. rope for the handle, 2 in. finishing nails, white glue, and two pieces of plastic laminate for the sides, 22 x 7-1/2 in. each.

Cut sides 22 in. long and ends exactly 14 in. wide. Draw a line 3/8 in. in along the bottom outside of the ends and sides to mark where you will nail. Also draw a line 1 in. from the inside ends of the sides so you'll know where to position the end board. Lay one of the sides down on a flat surface and start hammering three nails 1-3/8 in. in from the ends until the points are just barely poking out through the back side.

Rest the two ends upright against a wall (with the bottom in between them) and after laying down a bead of white glue on all

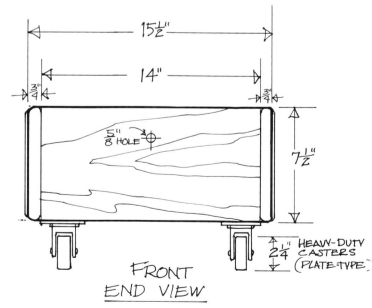

FRONT
END VIEW

PORTABLE STORAGE WAGON

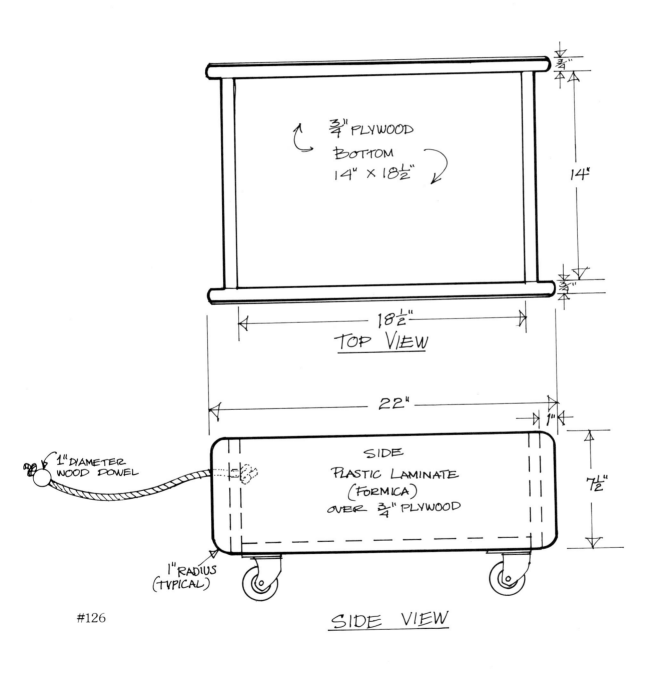

$\frac{3}{4}$" PLYWOOD
BOTTOM
14" X 18$\frac{1}{2}$"

$\frac{3}{4}$"

14"

$\frac{3}{4}$"

18$\frac{1}{2}$"

TOP VIEW

22"

1"

SIDE
PLASTIC LAMINATE
(FORMICA)
OVER $\frac{3}{4}$" PLYWOOD

7$\frac{1}{2}$"

1" DIAMETER
WOOD DOWEL

1" RADIUS
(TYPICAL)

#126

SIDE VIEW

PORTABLE STORAGE WAGON

joints, nail the sides onto the ends (see illus. #127). Do the same for the other side, making sure the bottom fits snugly. Then nail the sides and ends to the plywood bottom. Before driving the nails all the way, check to see that everything is positioned correctly. Recess the finishing nails below the surface of the wood by hammering them down with a nail set (see page 15). Fill the nail holes with wood filler and sand the surface smooth.

To protect the sides from nicks and mars, cover them with plastic laminate. A piece this small can be glued on with white glue instead of contact cement. Spread the glue over both sides with a flat piece of cardboard, and evenly press them overnight using heavy weights or clamps (see illus. #128).

When the glue has dried, trim off the plastic laminate (see page 8) and round off the edges with a file and sandpaper. Bore a hole in the front end for the rope handle. Thread one end of the rope through, tying a stop knot at the end. Bore a hole in a 4 in. long x 1 in. diameter wooden dowel and tie the other end of the rope to it.

Paint the interior and exterior ends of the toy bin with three coats of polyurethane. Attach the casters, and your child and toys are ready to roll.

Casters come in many sizes and styles. The most common type available are the white nylon casters sold in most variety stores. Make sure the casters are at least 2 in. so that they will go over rugs and door sills easily. Casters come in two basic shapes, plate or stem (see illus. #129).

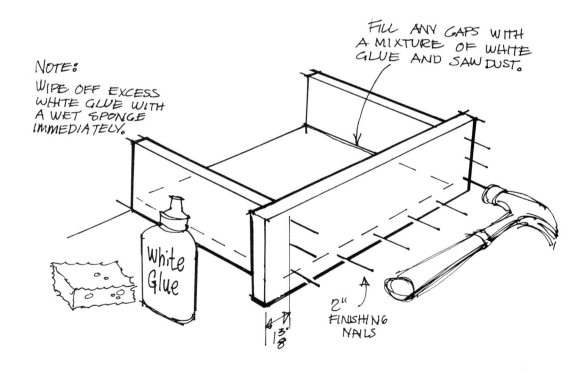

NOTE:
WIPE OFF EXCESS WHITE GLUE WITH A WET SPONGE IMMEDIATELY.

FILL ANY GAPS WITH A MIXTURE OF WHITE GLUE AND SAW DUST.

White Glue

2" FINISHING NAILS

#127

PORTABLE STORAGE WAGON

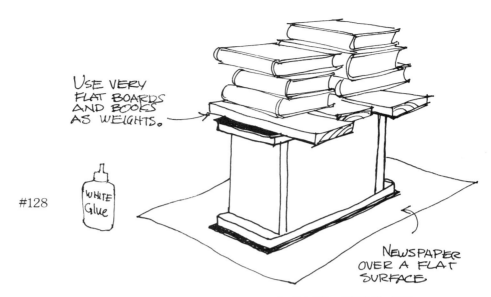

USE VERY
FLAT BOARDS
AND BOOKS
AS WEIGHTS.

WHITE
GLUE

#128

NEWSPAPER
OVER A FLAT
SURFACE

CASTERS— CASTERS COME IN MANY SIZES AND STYLES.
THE MOST COMMON ARE THE WHITE NYLON CASTERS
SOLD IN MOST VARIETY STORES.

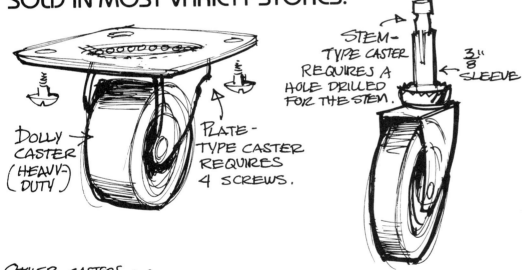

DOLLY
CASTER
(HEAVY-
DUTY)

PLATE-
TYPE CASTER
REQUIRES
4 SCREWS.

STEM-
TYPE CASTER
REQUIRES A
HOLE DRILLED
FOR THE STEM.

$\frac{3}{8}$" SLEEVE

OTHER CASTERS
ARE DESIGNED
FOR RUGS
AND HAVE
FLAT
ROLLERS...

...OTHERS COME WITH
A BRAKE LEVER.

#129

SECTION 3: DESIGN IDEAS

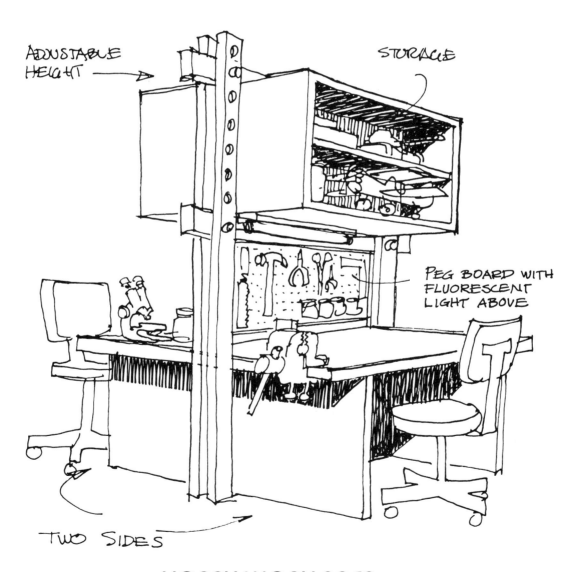

ADJUSTABLE HEIGHT

STORAGE

PEG BOARD WITH FLUORESCENT LIGHT ABOVE

TWO SIDES

#130

HOBBY WORK AREA

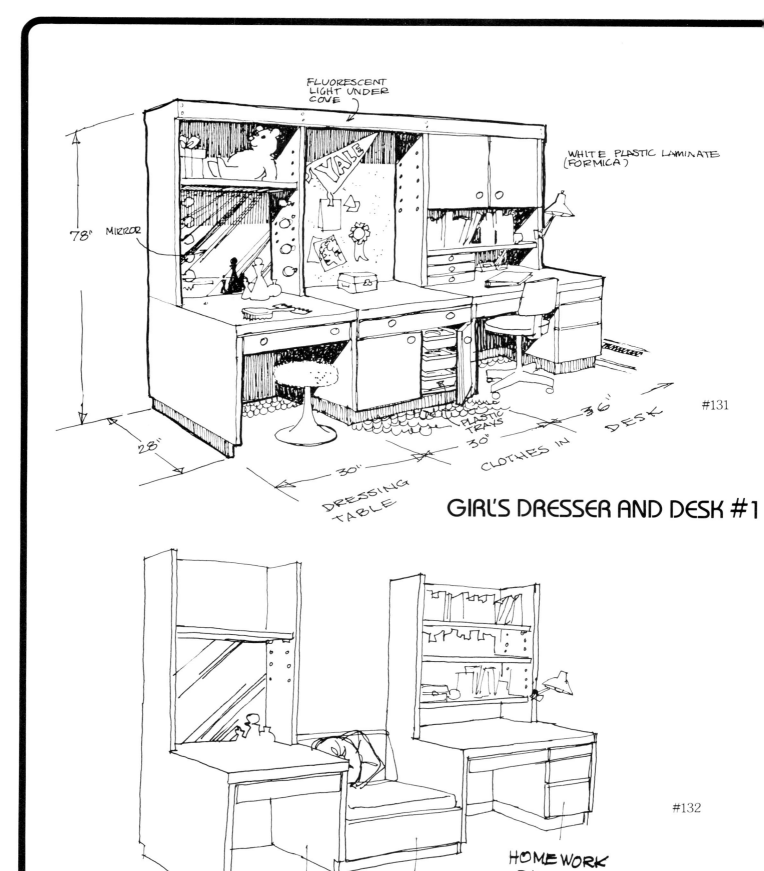

FLUORESCENT
LIGHT UNDER
COVE

WHITE PLASTIC LAMINATE
(FORMICA)

78"

MIRROR

28"

30"

30"

36"

CLOTHES IN DESK

PLASTIC
TRAYS

DRESSING
TABLE

#131

GIRL'S DRESSER AND DESK #1

#132

DRESSING
TABLE

COUCH

HOMEWORK
DESK

GIRL'S DRESSER AND DESK #2

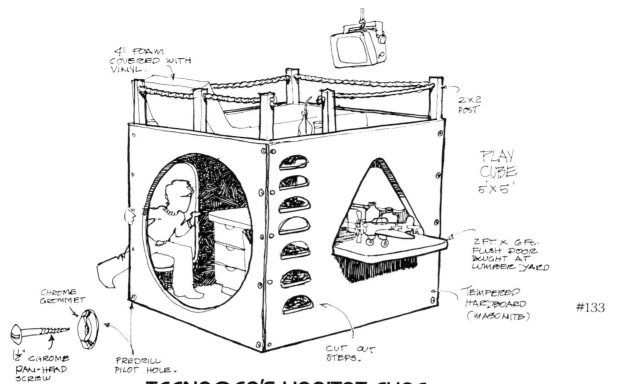

4" FOAM COVERED WITH VINYL.

2×2 POST

PLAY CUBE 5'×5'

2 FT. × 6 FT. FLUSH DOOR BOUGHT AT LUMBER YARD

#133

CHROME GROMMET

TEMPERED HARDBOARD (MASONITE)

1½" CHROME PAN-HEAD SCREW

PREDRILL PILOT HOLE.

CUT OUT STEPS.

TEENAGER'S HABITAT CUBE

MOM

#134

BUNK BEDS, DESK AND DRESSER

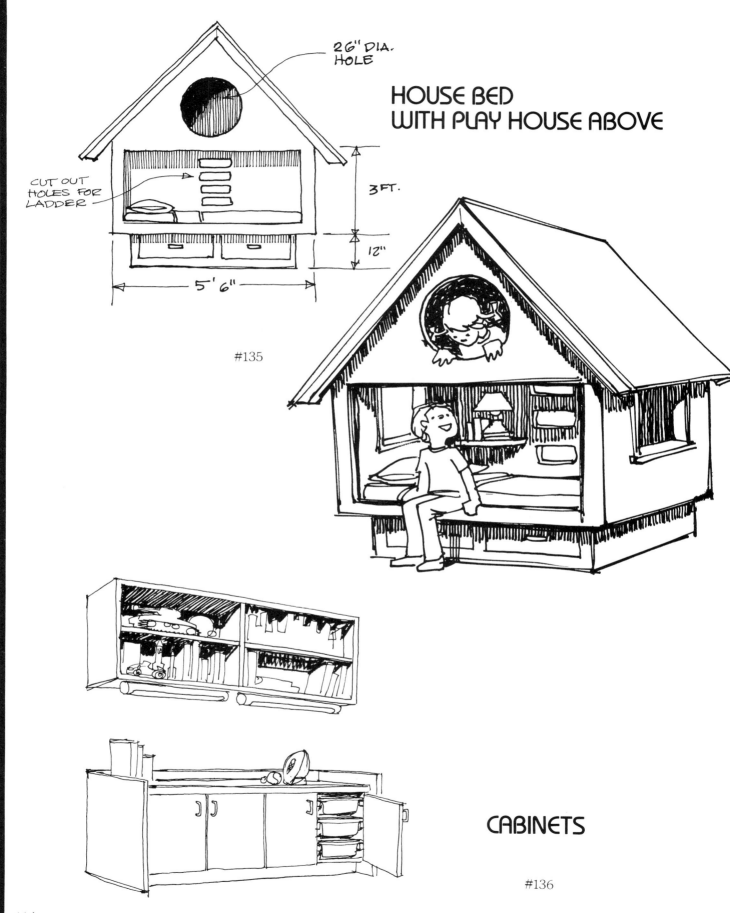

26" DIA. HOLE

HOUSE BED
WITH PLAY HOUSE ABOVE

CUT OUT HOLES FOR LADDER

3 FT.

12"

5' 6"

#135

CABINETS

#136

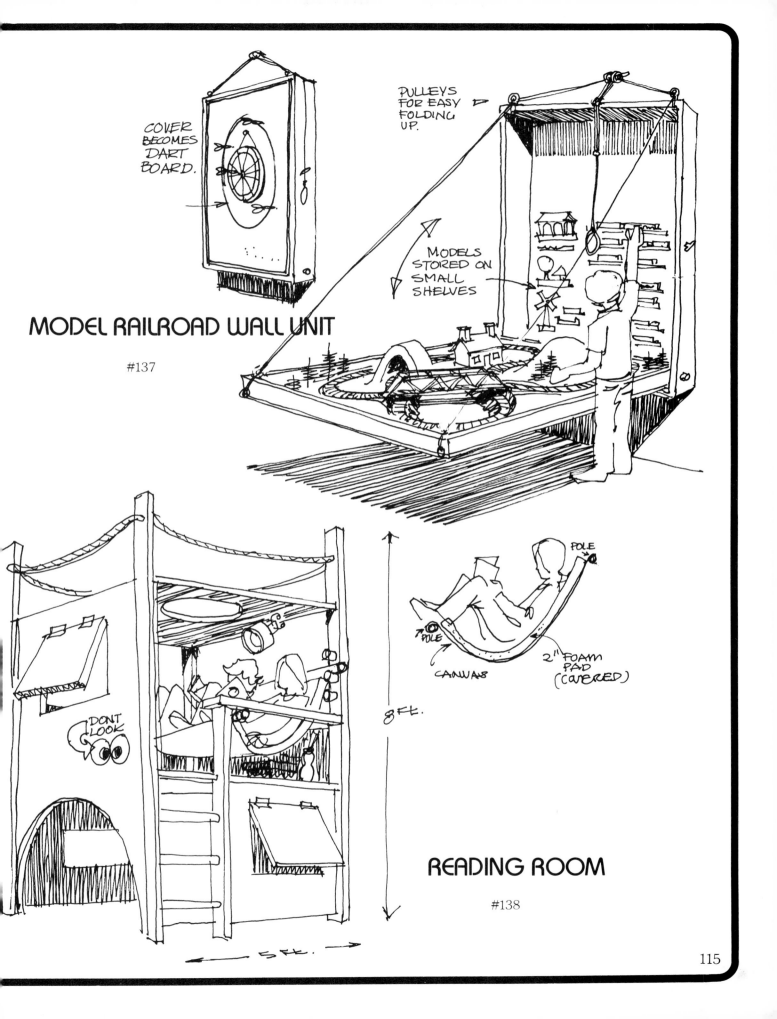

COVER
BECOMES
DART
BOARD.

PULLEYS
FOR EASY
FOLDING
UP.

MODELS
STORED ON
SMALL
SHELVES

MODEL RAILROAD WALL UNIT

#137

DON'T
LOOK

POLE

POLE

CANVAS

2" FOAM
PAD
(COVERED)

8 FT.

READING ROOM

#138

5 FT.

115

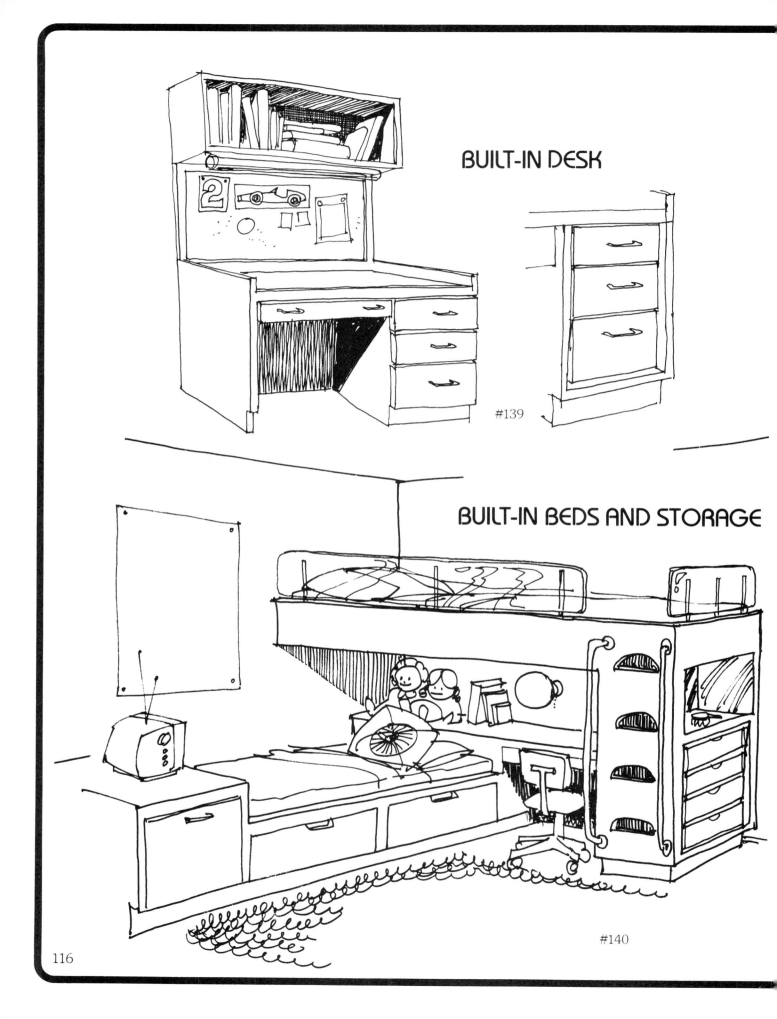

BUILT-IN DESK

#139

BUILT-IN BEDS AND STORAGE

#140

116

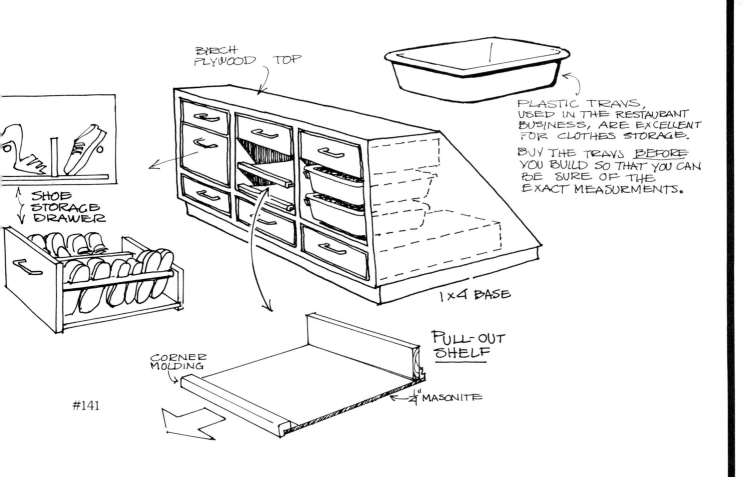

BIRCH PLYWOOD TOP

SHOE STORAGE DRAWER

PLASTIC TRAYS, USED IN THE RESTAURANT BUSINESS, ARE EXCELLENT FOR CLOTHES STORAGE.
BUY THE TRAYS BEFORE YOU BUILD SO THAT YOU CAN BE SURE OF THE EXACT MEASURMENTS.

1x4 BASE

PULL-OUT SHELF

CORNER MOLDING

¼" MASONITE

#141

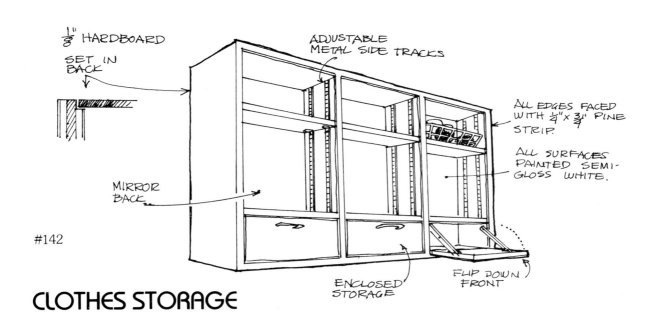

⅛" HARDBOARD

SET IN BACK

ADJUSTABLE METAL SIDE TRACKS

ALL EDGES FACED WITH ¼" x ¾" PINE STRIP.

ALL SURFACES PAINTED SEMI-GLOSS WHITE.

MIRROR BACK

#142

ENCLOSED STORAGE

FLIP DOWN FRONT

CLOTHES STORAGE

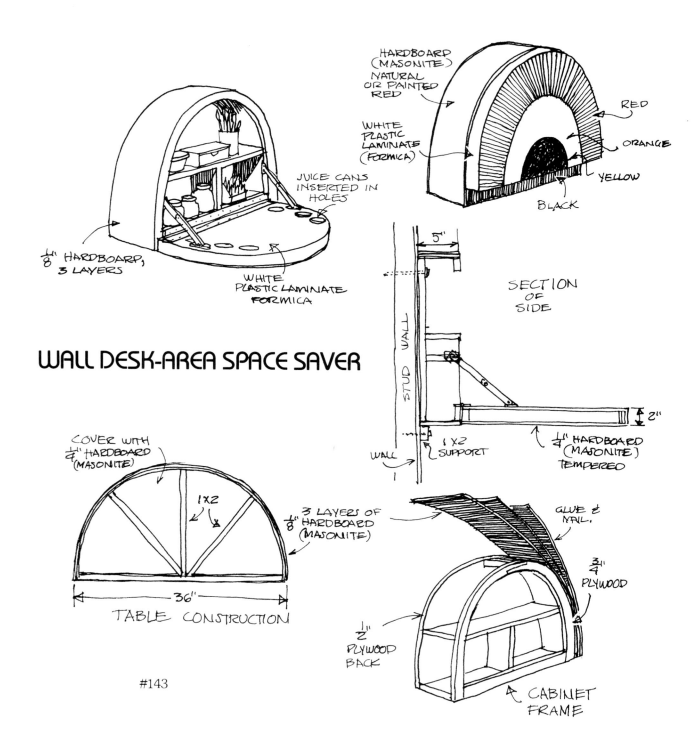

HARDBOARD
(MASONITE)
NATURAL
OR PAINTED
RED

WHITE
PLASTIC
LAMINATE
(FORMICA)

RED

ORANGE

YELLOW

BLACK

JUICE CANS
INSERTED IN
HOLES

$\frac{1}{8}$" HARDBOARD,
3 LAYERS

WHITE
PLASTIC LAMINATE
FORMICA

WALL DESK-AREA SPACE SAVER

5"

SECTION
OF
SIDE

STUD WALL

WALL

1 X 2
SUPPORT

2"

$\frac{1}{4}$" HARDBOARD
(MASONITE)
TEMPERED

COVER WITH
$\frac{1}{4}$" HARDBOARD
(MASONITE)

1 X 2

3 LAYERS OF
$\frac{1}{8}$" HARDBOARD
(MASONITE)

36"

TABLE CONSTRUCTION

#143

GLUE &
NAIL.

$\frac{3}{4}$"
PLYWOOD

$\frac{1}{2}$"
PLYWOOD
BACK

CABINET
FRAME

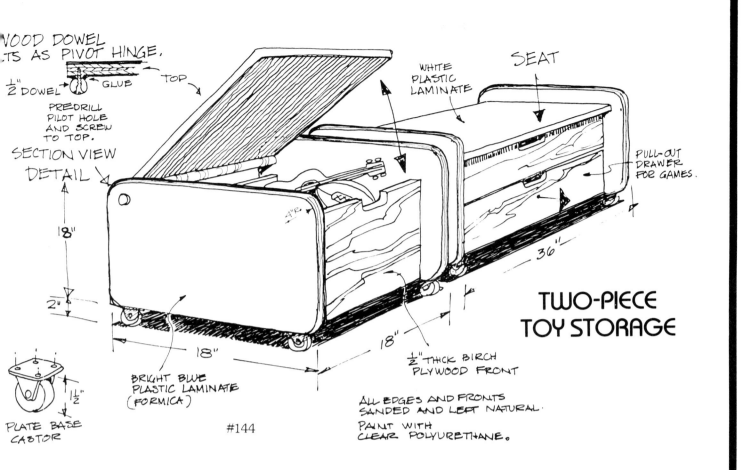

WOOD DOWEL
ACTS AS PIVOT HINGE.

$\frac{1}{2}$" DOWEL — GLUE — TOP

PREDRILL
PILOT HOLE
AND SCREW
TO TOP.

SECTION VIEW
DETAIL

18"

2"

PLATE BASE
CASTOR

$1\frac{1}{2}$"

BRIGHT BLUE
PLASTIC LAMINATE
(FORMICA)

18"

#144

WHITE
PLASTIC
LAMINATE

SEAT

PULL-OUT
DRAWER
FOR GAMES.

36"

18"

$\frac{1}{2}$" THICK BIRCH
PLYWOOD FRONT

TWO-PIECE TOY STORAGE

ALL EDGES AND FRONTS
SANDED AND LEFT NATURAL.
PAINT WITH
CLEAR POLYURETHANE.

HARDWARE

#145

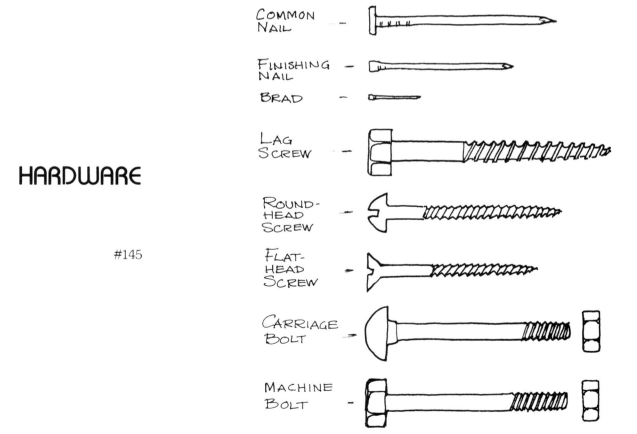

COMMON NAIL —

FINISHING NAIL —

BRAD —

LAG SCREW —

ROUND-HEAD SCREW —

FLAT-HEAD SCREW —

CARRIAGE BOLT —

MACHINE BOLT —

David Stiles is known for his other "do-it-yourself" books, FUN PROJECTS FOR DAD AND THE KIDS, HUTS AND HIDEAWAYS, and THE TREE HOUSE BOOK and has appeared on television in demonstrations and interviews. His projects have been featured in *House Beautiful, American Home, Popular Mechanics,* and *New York Magazine.* Recently he won two awards from the New York City Planning Commission for his designs of a playground for disabled children.